# Getting About in the
## Great Outdoors

Packed with practical advice and hints on preparation, safety, equipment and techniques, from the most basic to the very sophisticated, and with lively action drawings, here is a book that shows the complete novice – as well as the more experienced person – how to get the most out of the Great Outdoors, whether it's far away, or even on your doorstep.

The contents include hill walking, fell running, orienteering, cross-country skiing, cycling and cyclo-cross, rock and ice climbing, potholing, hang gliding, the 'ropes confidence' courses of adventure schools, all forms of camping from a tent to a snow-hole, and water activities such as sailing, board-sailing, white water canoeing and even rafting. A book for anyone drawn by the call of adventure, and one that will lure even the most timid out into the Great Outdoors.

Anthony Greenbank is a former Outward Bound instructor who has written many books for young people on camping, survival and climbing, and who devotes much of his time to climbing and mountaineering.

Anthony Greenbank

# GETTING ABOUT
## IN THE GREAT OUTDOORS

*Illustrated by Andrew Skilleter*

KESTREL BOOKS

*For Heather, Mark and Hannah*

KESTREL BOOKS
Published by Penguin Books Ltd
Harmondsworth, Middlesex, England

Copyright © 1984 by Anthony Greenbank
Illustrations Copyright © 1984 by Andrew Skilleter

First published in 1984

Typeset, printed and bound in Great Britain by
Hazell Watson & Viney Limited,
Member of the BPCC Group, Aylesbury, Bucks

British Library Cataloguing in Publication Data

Greenbank, Anthony
Getting about in the great outdoors.
1. Outdoor recreation – Handbooks,
manuals, etc.
I. Title
796      GV191.6

ISBN 0–7226–5803–6

# Contents

# *Foreword*

## by Chris Bonington

I am delighted Tony Greenbank has written this book. 'Coronation Street' in Cheddar Gorge and, recently, 'Point Five Gulley' on Ben Nevis are typically magic climbs we have done together.

Rock and ice climbing are only two of the options presented here. But I know Tony has been in good hands with the experts who helped him write on kindred activities like hang gliding and windsurfing.

The opportunities for open-air adventure are wide open as never before if you are young, or young at heart. This is because equipment today is excellent, while the broad-based choice of courses available offer additional safety.

Tony wraps all these aspects into a most appealing book. I wish it had been there when I was a boy.

# Acknowledgements

I would like to thank all the experts who suggested alterations to the illustrations and text of the book (any remaining errors are mine), particularly Colin Mortlock, director of Outdoor Education, Charlotte Mason College of Education.

Also Sam Crymble and Tim Walker of Glenmore Lodge, Alan Evans, Ben Lyon, Nick Mortimer, John Porter, Andy Hislop, Jim Whitworth, David Weeks, Nick McGill, Peter Chilvers and John Hillaby.

Thanks are also due to Outward Bound, Eskdale, for allowing me to borrow information on 'lifting a compass bearing', and to Stan Johnston (Border Liners) who kindly allowed me to use his orienteering map of Eycott Hill.

# 1

## How to Make the Outdoors Great

This book should be of immediate practical use to any young person attracted by the excitingly different outdoor activities which we are now so keenly made aware of, particularly through television.

Hang gliding, cross-country skiing, rock climbing on the specially built climbing walls of gymnasiums and sports centres, windsurfing on the waters of gravel pits, canoeing on any water from canals to raging rivers, ice climbing on frozen waterfalls near the roadside: to take part in activities such as these is within anybody's scope now. And they have that extra spice of danger which is so far removed from tamer activities like cricket, football or tennis.

This is not to say that football, cricket or tennis don't have their dangerous moments. Anyone who has faced up to fast bowling or been brought down by someone hard in a tackle, or who has been hit in the eye by a tennis ball, knows otherwise.

It's just that in the great outdoors the experience can be much more prolonged. You are far more remote from other people up a mountain or on the sea than ever you are likely to be in the park or on regatta water, where in moments you can be whisked away in an ambulance if things go wrong.

So to keep well out of the way of rescue services, helicopters and off-shore rescue boats I suggest you take advantage of the wealth of outdoor pursuit courses now available. Many of them teach you indoors on simulated rock faces, sailboard trainers or hang-glider control bars, and there are swimming-pool sessions for canoeists. Some of these courses are not

even residential and can be found locally. Residential ones, at Glenmore Lodge or Outward Bound centres, will give you an even bigger bonus in terms of techniques learnt thoroughly, and you won't form any of those bad habits so easily picked up without proper instruction. And what you've learnt will give you a greater margin of safety.

At the end of this book are addresses of organizations who will gladly send you details of various adventure courses and tell you where to find the nearest clubs specializing in activities such as rock climbing and canoeing. So that's the first step in the great outdoors indoors. The next? Learn the basics on a course and then try some easy trips with friends – hill walking, climbing or sailing. The choice is wide open.

# 2

## The Great Outdoors
## Indoors

Suppose you have not yet made up your mind what you really want to do outdoors? That's no problem. There are all kinds of ways people become interested. All you need for now is an open mind and a willingness to try something new and different.

### READING UP

First do some reading to get a few ideas of where to go. These are useful – *The Times Atlas of the World: Comprehensive Edition* has an excellent gazetteer which pinpoints any place you might want to find on maps, like the Old Man of Hoy rock pinnacle in the Orkneys, for instance.

Another key reference is the *ABC Coach Guide*, which lists all mainline bus services in Britain. Your local library will have local bus and rail timetables.

Local street maps will be in the reference library in case you are planning a street orienteering event, so will large-scale Ordnance Survey maps.

The 25-ins.-to-a-mile maps (used by surveyors and architects) can help locate rougher terrain on the outskirts of the town or city where you live which may be ideal for trying out camping, orienteering, Nordic skiing and so on.

Look at some outdoor magazines too, like *Climber & Rambler*, *The Great Outdoors*, *Yachting World*, *Foot-Loose*, *Camping*, *Mountain*, *Canoe Focus*, *High* or the *National Geographic*.

Find out the names of shops selling outdoors equipment in

the area – real clearing houses of information in themselves and places where young climbers, canoeists, potholers and the like gather. A good climbing shop, for instance, will put you in touch with the local climbing scene, where beginners are usually only too welcome.

Ask at your local library for the names and addresses of secretaries of local outdoor clubs, and of national organizations such as the British Canoe Union, the British Mountaineering Council and the Austrian Alpine Club.

## TUNING YOURSELF UP

The best way to get fit for rock climbing, white water canoeing or hang gliding is to cliff-hang, paddle or fly as much as you can. The more you do, the more you build up the muscles and fitness required as well as the right mental attitude. You don't really notice the aches and pains – well, not quite as much – because you are doing something you enjoy rather than just a series of exercises.

However, there is another way of looking at it. Supposing you were suddenly given the opportunity to go rock climbing with an expert in a month's time? Or your school or firm give you the chance to go on an Outward Bound course within a month or two? Wouldn't it make sense to tune up any part of yourself you might feel was somewhat lacking – say your arms or, indeed, your arms, legs and stomach muscles if you feel a fuller servicing is needed?

Victorian mountain climbers in Britain, the men who started rock climbing as a sport in its own right, pumped their muscles up with barbells – advance preparations still followed today by young climbers with an eye on the steepest and hardest rock climbs of all.

It has been the 'done thing' for some time to follow a set of pre-ski exercises a few weeks before taking a skiing holiday. This reduces the risk of broken legs and makes it easier for you in the long run.

Rather than lay down any hard and fast rules, I'd prefer to

leave it with you. If you feel your arms and stomach muscles are wimpy, there's no need to invest in a Bullworker – good as the Bullworker is. Any good library book on getting fit will give you workouts to do using sit-ups, press-ups and chin-ups as basic muscle builders. Hanging by the fingertips from a door lintel is a good isometric exercise for the arms.

I will suggest one exercise, however. It has been used by the hard men of rock climbing for many years and is none the worse for that. It's known as the wrist-roller.

Drill a hole through a short length of broom handle. Thread and knot the end of a 1-metre length of strong cord through this hole. Then tie a small heavy object to the end of the cord. It could be an old electric iron or a bottle full of sand or (heavier still) coffee grounds.

Grasp the pole, arms bent at 90° and elbows held in to your sides, palms downwards, and wind the weight slowly up and down.

Do this until you are tired. When the exercise becomes easier, substitute a heavier weight. You can also prolong the raising and lowering of the weight, and you might like to try it with both arms held out straight.

How your fingers, wrists and forearms will cry for mercy! It is the one thing that tells you your training is doing some good.

Weight training works on the principle that you wreck your muscle fibres so that they will gradually grow stronger in between exercise sessions. Blood floods the worked-over muscle and builds strong new tissue out of the wreckage.

It really helps if you can compete against someone else doing the same workout. This tends to keep you going longer without stopping. It also brings out the best in you when it comes to that final squeezing out of effort which is when the muscles start to benefit (though you may feel it's killing you at the time).

Solo exercising can be boosted if you count your 'reps' (repetitions) and try to improve on them, but beware over-doing things. Serious weight trainers work out on alternate days to give their muscles a chance to recuperate in between.

## KEEPING COMFORTABLE IN THE GREAT OUTDOORS

A brutal fact of life in the great outdoors is that if you aren't comfortable you may not be safe either. The two tend to go hand in hand.

Your first aim should always be to feel comfortable, even when caught in a storm at sea or so much rain that you look like a drowned rat. It is possible to feel at ease in the worst weather so long as you know your margins of safety and how to compensate for the hostility of the elements by wearing the right things.

Let's look at how our body functions in cold, wet weather. Hypothermia, or exposure, is the biggest killer on British hills – a surprise to many people who imagine it to be rock-climbing accidents or lightning-strike fatalities. Hypothermia means simply the progressive chilling of the body and it is deadly because it can so easily take you by surprise. Most cases of exposure on our hills take place in summer when the weather changes without warning and you aren't likely to be as well prepared for bad weather as in winter.

By rights the middle of your body should be warm like the soup or coffee inside a vacuum flask. This core of warmth acts as the body's central heating system. It is fuelled by the food you eat and the drink you swallow as well as by the action of your muscles as you move (under average conditions muscles produce enough heat to boil a litre of freezing water every hour).

Heated blood is pumped out towards the skin by the heart to help keep the surface of your body warm too. This is difficult if you are wearing sodden clothes, made even chillier by the wind. The body's core then becomes cool, colder-than-usual blood returns to the skin and there grows colder still. You become a kind of refrigerator turning chillier and chillier. If this isn't stopped in time, your heart gives up.

The trouble with hypothermia is that it plays serious tricks with the brain from its onset. The victim may not realize just how cold he really is, and he isn't in a position to know what's happening deep inside him. So it makes sense to foresee this possibility and take the right clothing with you in the first place. This, plus the right food and the company of friends, is the way to escape the risks of exposure.

It is also easy to get too hot. This again is something you may not realize until you drop with exhaustion. You could be in a position where, because of the weather, it is imperative you keep going as night is drawing in or a storm approaching. Imagine your muscles toiling away to brew all those innumerable mugs of steaming hot tea (in theory, that is!) on a reasonably mild day. And are you still wearing an anorak? Or a sweater? This will make you far too warm. What you need are several thin layers of clothing which can be regulated to the particular climate of the day. You take off layers when you feel too warm and replace them when you stop moving or begin to shiver.

Thin sweaters, shirts, T-shirts, sweat shirts and vests are better any day than thick and bulky sweaters. Not only are they more comfortable, since you can strip off or dress up as the weather dictates, but it is also easier to dry several thin layers than one thick one if need be.

There is another advantage, based on the fact that a layer of still air (unlike metal, say) is a poor conductor of heat. A teaspoon left standing in a cup of hot cocoa will quickly transmit heat whereas heat can only 'crawl' through air. It follows that a layer of air will help prevent your body warmth escaping on a cold day, and with several such layers surrounding you like onion skins not even the roughest weather will make a dangerous impression on you.

A final, most important point is the need to wear a 'shell' of waterproof clothing over your layers to keep them dry. Damp clothing cancels out the benefit of the 'dead-air' layers as water, unlike air, is an efficient conductor of heat. Wet layers of clothing are only ten per cent as efficient at preserving your body heat as the same layers dry. It's rather the same as seeing a pound note or dollar bill turning into a ten-pence or dime coin whenever it gets wet.

Thin wool sweaters are better than those made from

artificial fibres. Wool retains air between the fibres quite efficiently even when wet. This is also why woollen hats and gloves are warmer on a cold, wet day than synthetic ones. Remember that as much as a third of the body's heat can escape through the top of the head when it is unprotected. Hill farmers have been known to catch pneumonia after attending funerals in mid-winter, as they're not used to standing bare-headed.

## CLOTHING FOR THE GREAT OUTDOORS

The following are useful for any kind of outdoor activity and in everyday life as well. If by some chance you give the great outdoors a rest and turn to something else, you won't have wasted your money.

## THERMAL UNDERWEAR AND TRACK SUIT BOTTOMS

A long-sleeved thermal vest, a pair of thermal long john underpants and a pair of track suit bottoms (sold in outdoor shops and department stores separately from track suit tops) form the basis of modern adventure clothing and are indispensable for a number of outdoor activities. In cold weather you wear all three; in warmer conditions, just the track suit bottoms along with appropriate warm weather gear.

### SHORTS

The kind of shorts worn by joggers and runners are fine for summer. The freedom of movement they give, for example when rock climbing, is fantastic. If you still require this freedom of movement in cooler weather, you can wear your shorts over your thermal long johns. True, you look a bit like Superman, but this is exactly what fell runners wear when racing on winter's mountains in organized events.

## OVER-TROUSERS

Lightweight waterproof trousers – 'rain pants' in America – are necessary reserve clothing in case you meet bad weather. You also wear them from the start if going ice climbing. They fold into a small weightless package.

## T-SHIRTS, SWEAT SHIRTS AND SHIRTS

Layers of shirts – together with your thermal vest – provide just the kind of warmth you need and are much better than sweaters. You may own them already, so you can save on a possible expense here.

## CAGOULE

A 'cag' is a knee-length hooded anorak, preferably zipped or press-studded all the way up the front. Thin waterproof nylon, the most popular material for cags, unfortunately lets water vapour from your body's exertions condense on the inside, and you can end up getting wetter as a result of sweating than from the rain outside. You must therefore be able to ventilate your cag by unfastening it whenever the rain slackens. A loose fit and large pockets help too.

## THERMAL JACKET

Fibre pile clothing is popular enough to be a fashion on sale everywhere from filling stations to supermarkets as well as stores catering for the great outdoors. The soft brushed nylon fur on the inside retains a layer of insulating air, but you need a shell to keep you warm in windy weather.

## HAT AND GLOVES

Ski hats are good. So are thin thermal face-mask balaclavas – the sort that fold easily into a pocket.

SOCKS

Loop-stitched ankle socks go with thermal long johns and track suit bottoms, and can be worn comfortably with your ordinary shoes all year round.

FOOTWEAR

The best footwear for most activities in this book is a pair of good fell running shoes. These are expensive training shoes with the kind of ribbed and studded sole that grips just about everywhere, and are fine for mountain walking, gorge walking and scrambling, cycling, orienteering and basic rock climbing.

The soles are so efficient that some people like to save them from being worn away too quickly by walking in a pair of ordinary trainers to the spot where fell running shoes are needed and then switching to the more rugged pair.

If you get them wet, it's no real problem. The loop-stitched ankle socks I have mentioned feel warm even when wet. You won't suffer serious damage provided you are not walking on snow and you change into dry trainers and socks as soon as possible.

Two things are almost certain: trainers dry out quickly and they won't blister your feet as often happened with the heavy leather boots used by outdoor fans in past years.

For serious backpacking over mountains and moors (though I opt for fell running shoes every time) many people, including Outward Bound and most other outdoor pursuits centres, prefer altogether more substantial boots. These guard against the risk of going over on your ankle and protect your feet from sharp rocks, scree, stream beds, holes and other pitfalls of exacting cross-country terrain.

Fortunately modern mountain walking boots are lightweight and fairly waterproof and you can use them all year round and wherever the going is rough. They are made from lightweight leather with a rubber sole patterned or a mixture of leather and a hard-wearing footwear fabric that dries quickly and can be proofed so they shouldn't absorb water.

Footwear for the great outdoors in winter, to be worn in muddy or snowy conditions, is another thing altogether. Lightweight boots which are flexible are unsuitable for crampons. Also they quickly get wet and feet inside can freeze. Traditional leather mountain boots, heavy and expensive, and which need breaking in, are no longer considered viable for winter climbing or walking. In their place has come the plastic boot. Totally rigid, it is made like a ski boot, with a plastic shell surrounding a thick layer of padding or a complete inner boot lacing high and resembling the kind of boot boxers wear in the ring. You can wear these inner boots like slippers, leaving the outer 'shells' by the tent or hut door.

The boots are light and totally waterproof (unless you go in over the ankle when crossing streams). They are tailor-made for crampons, the metal spikes on frames which climbers attach to the soles of their boots for serious winter – and particularly ice – climbing.

Look out for walking boots made using the same system of an impervious outer shell with luxurious padding inside. By the time this book is published they may be in the shops.

Remember that you may need a variety of footwear for one trip. At the foot of the rock face a climber may change from boots or training shoes into rock-climbing shoes – lightweight, tight-fitting, as smooth-soled as a racing car tyre and designed to adhere to the smallest rock wrinkle.

These are specialist shoes, of course. Just as potholers wear a short wellington boot with the kind of moulded rubber sole used by climbers, cross-country skiers use a special lightweight Nordic ski boot, and the cyclo-cross expert might prefer a cycling shoe, you can only work out the footwear possibilities for yourself by taking part in and actually learning the activities which appeal to you.

## FOOD

To enjoy the great outdoors to the fullest you must keep alert, and food is a great help towards this. Next to the right clothing it's your best defence against exposure, and in winter it's the priority.

Bars of chocolate, packets of crisps, bags of peanuts and raisins, slabs of Kendal mint cake, chunks of fruit cake, wodges of flapjack, slices of bread buttered and jammed, a tin of fruit salad, packs of barley sugar, liquorice-allsorts or other sweets and cans of soft drinks – these are fine.

Aim to keep up your energy (and spirits) continually during an energetic day in the wilds. Nibbling, chewing and drinking work wonders. Nowhere is this more noticeable than in winter when you need foods high in starch like honey sandwiches. High calorific food generates warmth to combat the cold, and a vacuum flask of hot soup or coffee helps.

## OTHER EQUIPMENT

### DAY SACK

A small rucksack or 'day sack' is all you require now. Later you will need a full-sized sack for weekends and holidays, but you could still take your day sack along inside it, ready for day-to-day trips where only a minimum load is needed.

A day sack is a small bag with flat, well padded shoulder straps, comfortable even on bare shoulders, and a flap on top sometimes containing a zipped pouch. Choose one lined with plastic foam padding to prevent sharp objects inside bumping against your spine.

The climber's day sack will carry your thermal underwear (in case the weather turns nasty), shorts, T-shirts, over-trousers, cagoule, food and a spare pair of training shoes. It should have loops on the outside for securing ice axe and crampons if climbing is your aim.

Packed very lightly and fastened at waist level with a belt

attachment, a day sack can be carried on the back when cycling to the start of some walk, climb or run.

## COMPASS, MAP, MAP CASE AND WHISTLE

It makes sense to carry these four items which, between them, will ensure you don't get lost or at least don't remain lost too long!

The best kind of compass is the type made by Silva or Suunto. It will literally hand you direction-finding on a plate: the compass card and magnetic needle rotate on top of a small rectangular plastic plate on which is engraved a Direction of Travel arrow. You check from the map which way you want to go and adjust the plate accordingly. Then, turning your body around, you stop when the red tip of the magnetic needle hovers above North on the card below. You now walk, ski, pedal, paddle or fly where the Direction of Travel arrow is pointing.

The Ordnance Survey publish a most attractive choice of maps. The 1:50,000 sheets, for instance, will cover the region you want and give you all the information you need.

A map case keeps your map dry, clean and folded in the right places. You can see where you are at a glance without having to unfold a large piece of paper in the wind. Keep a red ballpoint pen in the map case, as red shows up well if you are drawing in connecting lines between points you wish to visit. A route card can also be kept here.

A cheap plastic whistle worn on a string around the neck – some people attach the compass to this as well – will let others know if you are lost.

## FIRST-AID KIT

Everyone in the great outdoors should carry his own small first-aid kit. Royal Marines carry a shell dressing each (a dressing for a large wound) when in action. When one marine finds another injured, it is the casualty's shell dressing he uses rather than his own.

You need a small plastic box. Fill it with the following: a bandage, some lint, adhesive tape, stretch fabric Elastoplast, a small pair of scissors, safety pins, cotton wool, antiseptic ointment and a small thermometer.

## HEAD TORCH

A headlight which fits on your helmet or forehead, tied round the head by an elastic band, is a boon in winter. Excellent ones can be found in outdoor shops. Good ones are more expensive but are robust, and their switch mechanism is more foolproof and easier to use than cheaper ones.

## BIVI BAG

Everybody heading for wild country should take a survival or bivi bag. Made from heavy-duty polythene, such a lifesaving envelope will fold up small and weigh little, yet – opened out – it will shield you inside from head to foot and with a good overlap for safety's sake. If you are ever stranded in a cold and exhausted state on mountains or by some lonely river, pothole or coastline you can survive the night in such a bag whereas without it you might not.

# 3

## Gym in the Trees

Hundreds of thousands of young people attending outdoor pursuits centres such as Outward Bound know the thrill of swinging like Tarzan through high trees, because today trees in the grounds of adventure schools supplement the most modern gymnasiums. In sky-high foliage you find a sense of height and space and a variety of high-wire circus acts that just aren't possible indoors. The confidence you gain in testing your balance, agility and strength on a ropes course is a marvellous feeling.

Problems close to the ground are actually the trickiest, but you can try them again and again without injury until you have mastered the knack. Dizzily high problems look sensational but are easy. Height rather than technical difficulty is the challenge here.

Most adventure schools welcome visitors and if you are keen will often supply you with an instructor to take you round the ropes course and whet your appetite for the thrills and spills of the great outdoors.

### A D-I-Y ROPES COURSE TEST

Obviously you can't build a ropes course at home of the same extent or with the same in-built safety as those found at an outdoor centre.

These are made from the best (very substantial) hemp ropes. Wire cables take the strain at strategic points, tightened up by Land Rover. A system of tying around cleats may be used so the ropes can be slackened off last thing at night, then tautened the following morning. Trees are surveyed for rotten wood, bad branches and so on, and these chopped away. Soft, level landings are found under each obstacle where a fall is likely. There are also escape routes – blocks of wood screwed to trees so that anyone finding a high-level problem too much can climb back down by an easy route. And in case the escape route proves too difficult for someone who is genuinely frightened, a ladder and safety rope are always handy as a last resort.

There is one test, however, which you can make at home. It is more of a test of strength than anything and, if you persevere at it, it will make you hard as nails. It brings into play certain muscles not often called upon and will certainly prove a challenge to you and your friends.

You need a short length of strong rope, a sturdy limb on a tree and a piece of pipe 3–5 cm in diameter and 1–2 m long.

Tie one end of the rope round the tree branch, run it down through the pipe and tie a strong knot at the lower end. When the pipe is hanging it should be a metre clear of the ground and there should be 4 m clearance all round it. Make a final check that the knot is large enough to prevent the rope slipping through the pipe.

Because the hanging pipe is free to swing it is also extremely difficult to climb – much harder than you might think. It is therefore a good yardstick of how your muscles are developing, as you find you can climb it higher and higher. It will quickly toughen you up for the ropes course proper.

## THE ROPES COURSE

Ropes courses are usually a continuous linking of one problem to another. The idea is to go round the full circuit without touching the ground. The instructor goes first to show you how and to test the safety of each problem at the same time. Nervous? Then let those more agile and eager lead the way.

You can watch them, bringing up the rear in your own good time.

Old clothes are just the thing here. You need long trousers which do not restrict your legs when fully bending the knees, and perhaps one or two sweaters or layers of T-shirts under an anorak to help protect you from rope burn. This is especially true for the long diagonal slide and the regain. Plimsolls or training shoes are fine. Check the laces are properly tied and tucked out of the way. Leave your wrist-watch, rings and necklaces on the ground.

The secret of going round a ropes course successfully – even though you may be brought to earth now and then – is never to hurry. Doing things in a rush invariably leads to falls or needless frights that a more concentrated, calculated and careful approach would have avoided. Here goes then!

### INCLINED LOG

This is a popular opening obstacle because it gets you high off the ground without too much difficulty, though not without a little excitement. The log leans up against a tree and has footholds axed across it at intervals. These may slope on purpose to make for a more awkward climb.

The tendency is to feel you will topple over to either side the higher you ascend. Grasping the sides of the log with both hands, place the feet sideways on the axe-cuts. Each time you step up take your weight on the underside of the outside edge of the big toe. It makes you splay-footed but, by forcing your heels down, keeps you more in balance. This is the way you often place the feet when rock climbing.

### STIRRUPS

Stepping from the top of the inclined log you will be faced with any one of a number of medium-height obstacles. A series of rope stirrups with a wooden rung at the bottom of each is a favourite.

The stirrups are large enough to stand in and climb through.

They hang, one after the other, along a horizontal rope in much the same way as shirts on a washing line. They take on a life of their own as your weight comes on the wooden bar of each stirrup, causing them to stretch down, dance and sway like merry-go-rounds.

The secret is always to reach out and grab hold of the next stirrup with one hand, reaching as high as possible, before placing the instep of your foot on the wooden rung at its base.

Keeping a tight grip with your hand, bring your other foot over on to the ring. Then take your second hand off the stirrup you have just vacated and grasp the stirrup you are standing in. Repeat these moves to switch to the next stirrup.

If you are ever unable to reach the next stirrup in line, stretch a hand back out to the stirrup you last left and, by pulling on it, start yourself swinging. This will bring you nearer the stirrup you want. Then grasp it quickly.

The stirrups are among the most strenuous ropes course obstacles. They tend to come early on in the chain of problems while you still have some strength in your arms. There's no doubt they help to make you stronger.

TWITCHING LOG

A long log suspended just above the ground by ropes, this lives up to its name in no uncertain manner. A handline is provided but it is several metres too long. The answer is to coil it in one large loop and, holding this with both hands gripped tightly, cross to the far end of the log, leaning forward hard against the tension you have created in the handline with your loop of slack rope.

If, however, the loop grows smaller as you make the crossing (and this happens because the rope loop tends to slip through your straining fists), the gap between the log and the handline becomes too wide and you fall off. To prevent this happening, place both feet across the log and take little steps sideways. As you grasp the loop, make sure that the first hand to slide sideways never opens. Your other hand should only slide in the same direction when the first hand has slid and then stopped, and when it does slide to join the first hand it should remain part open until it almost touches the first hand. Then it must lock hard on the loop it is holding while the first hand continues on another tight-fisted slide in the direction you want to go.

This description may make the hand movements sound more complicated than they are, but you will see how easy it is if you try it first with a piece of string.

### LEOPARD'S CRAWL

Leading you yet higher, this diagonally ascending tramline of two thick ropes is a favourite of Army assault courses. Try to avoid lying on top of the ropes. You will be held back by too much friction. Instead stand clear of the ropes by going on all fours – arms straight as you hold a rope in each fist, and legs bent with feet placed sideways and toes pointing out – splayed out across the ropes. Take small steps and go slowly.

### POSTMAN'S WALK

Two horizontal ropes about 2 m apart and parallel span the gap to the next tree. Using the lower one as a foot rail for sideways steps and the upper one as a handline you move across the 5 m or so one limb at a time.

### DESCENDING A SMOOTH TREE TRUNK

You can wrap both arms around the tree and, hugging it with knees bent and gripping the trunk, slowly slide downwards. Lower your hands as much as you dare before each descending shuffle.

Watch out for protuberances or bumps you can rest your feet on to take your weight. These can later be used as handholds.

*Tension traverse*

TENSION TRAVERSE

A balancing act near ground level across a thick tightrope tied securely between two trees, the tension traverse requires an extra aid to make it possible for you. This comes in the form of a lightweight line tied to a branch high above the end of the tightrope which is your destination.

You stand on the tightrope ready to make the crossing. Someone on the ground hands you the line. It's all yours. All you have to do is teeter across.

The expert pushes himself, feet sideways across the rope once more, away from the tree to full arm's stretch. He's a metre along on his journey and still in balance! Now he pulls the handline taut and places it in his mouth. Biting hard with the teeth, he slides the hand nearest his destination up the handline and grips it tight. Next he quickly takes his other hand from the tree and grasps the handline about the level of his navel. His position for the rest of the tightrope crossing is all set.

There are two keys to success: pulling as high as possible during the crossing with the hand nearest your destination and, by leaning backwards supported by the handline, keeping it taut between your hands.

INCLINED LADDER

Step carefully on to the rung of this 45° ladder which pivots freely at the top where it reaches a tree branch about 5 m up.

The ladder has wire cable sides with rungs of metal tubing spaced at irregular intervals and all askew. Most unstable, it will tip at the slightest provocation. However, it is safer than it looks. If you capsize, hang on to the wire cables or rungs you happen to be holding until the ladder has turned over, then drop into the sand pit below.

The easiest way to climb the inclined ladder is to grasp the cables. Place your feet at the ends of the rungs where they join the cables. Avoid having both feet on the same rung at the same time. Adjust for balance by pressing down on one cable and pulling up on the other. The best sequence is hand, opposite foot, other hand, other foot, each moved one at a time.

## BURMA BRIDGE

Three thick ropes span the gap – sometimes as great as 30 m – from tree to tree. The bridge tends to be high up and is a challenging problem, but also safe.

Tread on the knots formed where the thinner ropes (acting as 'struts' along the two sides of the bridge) are tied to the bottom rope which is used for the feet. These struts give stability and prevent you falling through.

Hold a side rope in each hand, hooking your elbows over the outside if you feel nervous. You can also pull these side ropes close to your body for a feeling of extra security.

## FLEA'S LEAPS

It takes nerve to lose the considerable height you have gained by jumping back down to near ground level via a series of three or four small platforms, each one smaller than the last until the final one looks about the size of a postage stamp! This is a test of confidence and is easier than it appears.

Take your time. Aim for the centre of each platform and take a deep breath. Once you decide to go, go. Bend the knees on landing and pause before the next leap to take stock again . . .

## VERTICAL ROPE CLIMB

Stand on the large knot at the bottom of this 5 cm diameter rope which hangs from a strong branch about 8 m above. Trapping the rope between the heel of one foot and the instep of the other, and powering your ascent almost completely by the strength of your leg muscles, straighten your legs, reach higher up the rope, bend your knees, bring up your feet and trap the rope between them again, straightening your legs once more. And so on to the top.

## CAVING LADDER

A caving ladder may be an alternative way of gaining the height reached by the vertical rope.

Climb this with one training shoe toe and one heel on alternate rungs as you would go down a pothole. Both hands should grasp the rungs from behind.

## YARD ARM

Imagine that this high-level log lashed between two trees is a spar on a famous clipper ship of yesteryear, like the *Cutty Sark*. Then it was all in a day's work to traverse the rope line just beneath it while your hands grasped the top of the yard-arm itself (the large log). For greater safety, hold on to the handline running behind the log as you cross from one tree to the next.

This is one of the easiest obstacles, also sensationally placed.

## LONG DIAGONAL SLIDE

From 10–15 m up a high tree, a 5 cm diameter rope slants down to near ground level at an angle of 45°–60°. The slide down should be done sitting astride it, one foot tucked up behind you, toes hooked over the rope.

The trick is to keep the toes of the hanging leg pointed towards the ground all the time. This gives you a counter-weight – a kind of keel. It also helps if, the left leg being the hanging one, you lean your head down to the right side of the rope during your slide. Wear one or two extra layers of clothing to prevent your body suffering rope burn.

## BALANCE BEAM

A large long log is lashed between two trees, perhaps 3 m from the ground in places. The distance you have to wobble your way across is some 7 m and might be split into two balancing acts with a gap halfway.

It's tricky in rain, so make sure the soles of your shoes are free from mud before you start. Any flat part of the log should be treated as an 'island' and aimed for along your way. You can rest on these. It also helps to picture the log as if it were lying on the grass so that if you do make a mistake you simply step off on to the ground.

## SWING

Having successfully reached the other end of the balance beam, somebody will hand you a rope hanging from a high branch above the centre of a clearing among the trees.

Leap from the log, grasping the rope and possibly pulling yourself up it hand over hand for several centimetres on your pendulum swing to the other side of the clearing.

Here you may find either a net or a horizontal rope stretched out between trees about 4 m above the ground on which you need to do the regain. Either of these obstacles will be right in your flight path.

## NET

Turn a thigh sideways-on to the net as you approach it. Grab for the mesh, letting go of the rope immediately. If you are nervous punch an arm out straight, then crook the elbow to ensure you connect with the net. But do let go with the other hand so the rope is free to swing back out of the way behind you.

REGAIN (RECOVERY)

If, instead of the net, the horizontal rope faces you at the end of your Tarzan-like arc, then you will need to catch hold of it, hang from it, pull yourself up so that you can lie on top of it and then, doing the commando crawl (explained later), pull yourself along in this position to the safety of the nearest tree.

Many young people find the regain is the toughest ropes course obstacle, but it is much easier when you know how.

Catch hold of the rope first with one hand then, dropping the swing rope, the other. Hang down to full arms' stretch. Now alter the grip of both hands on the horizontal rope. They should come close enough to touch each other, but should face opposite ways.

Curl the feet up, hook both ankles over the rope and relax. Then change the grip of the hands so that the backs both face the same way – to your left (if you are right-handed) as you lie upside down like a sloth.

Think: 'Right armpit, right leg.' Pulling up on the arms, hook the right armpit over the rope in a somewhat awkward resting position. Free the right ankle from its position on top of the rope and beat the right leg down, straight, toe pointed and with all the strength you can muster. This will turn your body over so that you end up lying on top of the rope. With your right leg hanging down, toes pointed towards the ground and your left foot tucked on top of the rope supporting you, drop your head so that if it were loose it would fall to the ground on the other side of the rope.

The best place to practise the regain is on one of the lower-level horizontal ropes of the obstacle course, such as the leopard's crawl. If you make a mess of things, simply lower your feet to the ground.

You may find the upward curl too difficult to do when you are hanging by both hands from the rope. The easy way (cheating!) is to hook your right armpit directly over the horizontal rope while still hanging on until the very last second of the swing rope.

*The Swing*

*The Regain and Commando Crawl*

It helps to wear extra clothing below your anorak when tackling the regain. Thin clothing will not be sufficient to protect your armpit as you struggle to support yourself on it and then pivot over using it as a fulcrum. You could get a nasty rope burn if your body isn't padded.

### COMMANDO CRAWL

Lie comfortably on top of the horizontal rope, one leg hanging down straight (don't pull it back up or let it come up of its own accord or you'll roll over) and the other hooked up on the rope by the ankle behind you. Let your head hang down on the opposite side of the rope from your hanging leg.

Drag yourself hand-over-hand towards the tree securing the far end of the rope. The rear foot hooked over the rope can supply a good amount of push if you bend it and then straighten it.

Shin down the tree to the ground or whatever further obstacle awaits you.

# 4

## *Cross-country Walking, Skiing and Cycling*

Rambling, skiing and cycling across open countryside have something to suit most personalities.

Walking off the beaten track is great for those who hate to miss a trick. Move faster than five miles an hour and you lose most of the sense impressions that swirl around while you are out and about.

Nordic – or cross-country – skiing is for the fit and athletically inclined. You can ski virtually anywhere on cross-country skis – your local park, golf course or even the pre-rush-hour roads in the early morning after an evening's snowfall, and when there is no snow you can still train by roller-skiing. This is becoming increasingly popular, and areas in city centres like London and Glasgow have been partly closed to allow roller-ski racers to compete against each other around the streets.

How would you like to try cycling over rocks and bog, grass and heather, going hell for leather? Cyclo-cross sport gives great scope for those who hanker to test nerve, muscle and sense of balance regardless of cuts and bruises. You lug your bicycle up mountains and ride down them.

These three separate activities can be carried out in areas of great natural beauty – and that could be on your own back doorstep given a beautiful sunset or dawn. It's not just the hard physical exertion which can take your breath away during a quiet moment among such wonderful settings . . .

## SAFETY RULES FOR VENTURING INTO THE WILDS

Outward Bound students are asked to read a set of rules for their own comfort and safety. It's worth keeping them in mind for the activities in this chapter.

Basically the safety rules are as follows. Groups should be not less than four in number (if one person is injured this allows two to go for help and one to stay with the casualty). Groups should not split up unless in an emergency. Every student should carry a waterproof shell of cagoule and over-trousers, spare sweater, map and compass, whistle, first-aid pack, food and pencil and paper *plus* (from October–April) warm hat, gloves and torch. Jeans, overalls and light flannels are not warm enough unless supplemented by long underpants, pyjama trousers or other trousers. Shorts may be worn on hills in summer but warm trousers must be carried too. It is most important to keep a reserve of strength in each member of the group, and an ample amount of daylight to compensate for delays.

Finally headlined are these words: *In summary, stay with your group, and always keep reserves of clothing, food and strength.*

At Outward Bound schools someone always knows where you are heading, but freelance walkers, skiers and cyclists are out on a limb. It's only common sense then to have the simple back-up of letting people know your plans. If you have told someone where you are going and when you expect to arrive, then if anything serious happens to you on the way you have covered yourself. When you don't make an appearance the police can be informed and in turn alert the rescue team nearest to where you should be. Given these circumstances, everything usually ends happily.

What sometimes happens, however, is that people unthinkingly change their route, reach a different destination and forget to inform those to whom they gave a route card. When this happens rescue teams have been known to search in vain for days. You can imagine their reaction when they find out the truth. The thing to do given such a change of plan is to telephone those expecting you when you reach safety. If they aren't on the phone, then ring the police instead. That will put your mind at rest as they will contact your friends.

## THE COUNTRY CODE

Closing gates, not climbing stone walls, taking your litter home with you and watching out for the slightest fire risk in woodland areas are basic ways of behaving in the country-side.

There are several other points which, if you use common sense, will help smooth your path should you meet a farmer with a chip on his shoulder. Keep to paths across farm land. Keep your dog under proper control too – a farmer is legally entitled to shoot it if he considers it a threat to his livestock. Keep the water you meet en route clean (including drinking troughs for animals). And keep on the right-hand side of country roads and well into the side on blind bends.

## DRESSING FOR CROSS-COUNTRY TRIPS

Making sure that you never chill or overheat is one of the most crucial things you must do in the great outdoors. The medical expression is *thermo-homeostasis* (even temperature). Many people get it wrong.

In Chapter 2, I stressed the need for thin layers of clothing sandwiching dead-air layers in between. Feel cold and you add an extra layer or two. Feel warm and you can peel off again. As an example of what I mean, here is the system of 'climate control' I use when making a favourite mountain walk of mine from home and back. It takes from two to three hours and reaches a summit 2,541 ft high – Red Screes in the Lake District.

Say it is a cold December day with snow on the tops and a good forecast for settled weather. This means I start from cold, wearing fell running shoes, loop-stitched ankle socks, thermal long john underpants, a thermal long-sleeved vest, a T-shirt and a lightweight nylon cagoule. I also wear a pair of woollen gloves and a ski hat for the time being.

As the body warms up and the angle up a lane steepens, I take off the cagoule, re-zip it up the front, twizzle it round and round by both sleeves and knot it round the waist like a narrow belt. If I feel warmer I take off the hat and gloves too.

On the last third of my way up the mountain, the route steepens considerably. I may start over-heating immediately this happens so I take off the T-shirt, holding it in a hand as I climb. Then I begin to feel still hotter as my body is working so hard despite the frosty air and breath pluming from my mouth. I stop a moment, strip off the thermal vest (wearing it, like the cagoule, around the waist and with the sleeves tied in a reef knot in front) and replace it quickly with the short-sleeved T-shirt. It's all I need to reach the summit, then just below this (in case the wind is blowing on top) I swap back to the thermal vest next to my skin, slip the T-shirt back on top and replace my cagoule and hat and gloves ready to face the cooler air you can expect on mountain skylines.

Coming down the long sharp-edged ridge is far less effort and is also fanned by updraughts of air from the valleys below. I might keep the anorak on all the way back to the village at its foot, though if I decide to run down, my body will heat up so quickly again the cagoule may have to come off and be tied around my waist once more.

This is a very simple example. It's the one followed by top mountaineers who have been on Himalayan expeditions, by the best rock climbers who know the miles you sometimes have to tramp to reach remote cragfaces and by both fell runners and orienteers going all out to win.

## THE SECRET OF COMFORTABLE FEET

If you ever feel your feet are beginning to rub against the insides of your training shoes or boots, *stop*. It's worth carrying a small pair of scissors so you can cut off a generously-sized piece of the stretch-fabric Elastoplast you should have for such emergencies, and place it carefully over the reddened place on your skin. Immediately it will cut the chances of the skin developing into a blister, and even if it is too late, plaster it anyway. The thick padding of clean lint held securely in position over the area will still ease soreness.

## HOW TO READ A MAP

A map is a scaled, plan view representation on paper of what appears on the ground. It is always worth carrying. It makes all the difference between knowing more or less exactly where you are and an aimless kind of travelling in the hope you will eventually arrive.

### THE SCALE

This tells you how to compare the area shown on the map with the area of countryside it represents. You can judge distances simply by looking at the map after only a little time spent learning the ropes.

Most maps are now printed on a metric scale. The popular Ordnance Survey (OS) maps (or series) are those with a scale of 1:50,000 (meaning that one centimetre on the map stands for 50,000 centimetres or half a kilometre on the ground). Many people think more easily in terms of inches and miles (Americans, for instance), in which case the 1:50,000 maps each represent 1¾ inches on the map for one mile on the ground.

These maps show footpaths, but many walkers prefer a larger scale map that reveals more detail and a clearer picture of the countryside, so they buy the 1:25,000 maps. The 1:25,000 OS Outdoor Leisure maps for popular tourist districts are especially useful.

THE KEY

All OS maps have a clearly arranged key which explains the symbols printed on the paper. You use the key to pick out points that interest you (some maps have features that others lack).

THE NATIONAL GRID

The grid is a framework of artificial lines spaced at one 1- to 10-kilometre intervals depending on the map's scale. These help you judge distances more easily (one kilometre is about the same as 0·6 miles). More important, the grid gives a method of pinpointing any position you want on the map by a shorthand, or reference, number.

To do this, take the west edge of the kilometre square in which your point lies and read the large figures printed against the line or in the north and south margins. Then estimate the position of the point in its square in tenths eastwards. Now take the south edge of the same kilometre square in which your point lies and read the large figures opposite the line on the east and west margins. Then estimate in tenths the position of the point in its square northwards of this line.

You now have a six-figure map reference number accurate to within 100 metres of the immediate countryside where you happen to be – or want to be.

CONTOURS

Places of equal height above sea level are joined by contour lines. The key will tell you whether the spacing between contours is in feet or the metric equivalent. If unsure, you can divide metres by three to get the rough measurement in feet. The 1:50,000 maps, for instance, show contour values to the nearest metre but the vertical height between contour lines is still 50 ft.

Closely-spaced contours show steep slopes while widely-spaced ones indicate gentle slopes. A lack of contours means a plain, a river valley or a hilltop plateau.

Where contours bend round in a loop like fingerprint whorls, they indicate what at first glance could be either a spur or breast of hillside or a valley or hollow. To know the difference between the two – and to make the contour lines jump into the relief of the actual landscape in your mind's eye – check the contour heights printed at intervals on the paper. If the innermost figure is highest and the outermost lowest (1,750, 1,500, 1,250, 1,000) it is high ground or a spur. If the numbers go the other way round, the ground will be a valley or depression. An extra help to recognizing whether looped contours show a hill or a hollow is that a stream or river may lie along the length of the contours if it is a valley.

## SETTING THE MAP

A good eye for contour patterns comes with practice. It will show you promising viewpoints – check where closely-spaced contours give way to a few widely-spaced contours, or where closely-packed contours thrust out into a valley or plain. If no contours are marked, climb a church tower (with permission) or large tree to view the countryside from a better vantage point and to practise identifying landmarks in the distance on the paper in your hands.

Spread out the map, then fold it into quarters and use the quarter that shows the countryside immediately around you. If you have a map case rejig your folding so that the area concerning you fits neatly into the plastic window. Turn the map around like a piece of jigsaw puzzle and suddenly it will 'fit' in exactly the same way as if it were a piece missing from the landscape. You have now 'set the map'.

That church spire in the distance is in line with the tiny ball and cross (which the key says is the symbol used for church with spire); that radio or TV mast on the other side of a wood coincides with the position of the map symbol shaped

*Setting the map*
(artist's licence: you can't actually do this while hang gliding!)

like a wigwam (again correct according to the key), while the spread of trees also corresponds to the position of the green patch on the map from where you are viewing the landscape.

And so on. As more features of the scenery tally with where you find the symbols for them on the map, you not only know exactly where you are on the map but can also identify just about anything you see.

You can also tell – without a compass – which way is north. This is because today's maps are drawn to the north. Either on the key or in the margin of the map you may find a small diagram showing three arrows pointing up the map's length and labelled *True North*, *Grid North* and *Magnetic North*. Don't worry about these now. All you need to know is that so long as your map is set, then the topmost edge of it is pointing in a northerly direction.

## CROSS-COUNTRY WALKING

Knowing the secrets of controlling your own personal climate and also how to read a map are the basics of wilderness walking.

There are many other small things which will keep you comfortable and therefore safer, like always trying to keep your feet dry. If you have to wade in water, take your boots and socks off, replace the boots, cross to the other side, then – drying your feet and emptying your fell running shoes or boots – replace the dry socks and the boots before continuing on your way.

It is particularly important to keep your group together at all times. *The pace of the group should be the speed of its slowest member.* If he is having difficulty keeping up, he should go to the front where walking is easiest. On no account should he ever be left to trail along behind with an ever-widening gap developing between him and the rest of the group.

This can happen easily if anybody has to stop for a moment, say to tie a shoelace. By the time he is ready to carry on again, the others can have moved an unbelievable distance ahead. If one person stops then so should the others, especially in remote, rugged countryside.


## CROSS-COUNTRY SKIING

In January 1982, four instructors from Glenmore Lodge, the Scottish Sports Council's national outdoor training centre, made the first-ever crossing of Scotland on skis. They completed the fifty miles in 16½ hours across all kinds of terrain.

They skied uphill as well as down; they skied along the ice of the frozen-solid River Affric; then they skied the surface of Loch Affric itself. They also skied country lanes and gritted roads, and they skied by night.

Nordic or cross-country (X-C) skiing is the 'other' kind of skiing, quite different from the downhill type you see on television's 'World of Sport'. The two are as opposite as pole vaulting is from sprinting. When you ski X-C you ski up and across the snow as well as down.

In Norway X-C skiing is almost the national family sport. It caught on fast in the United States too and is becoming increasingly popular in Britain. One reason is that X-C skiing can be done at home. You can ski X-C wherever there is snow and you don't need much of that. A heavy frost will do.

X-C skiing is easy on the pocket into the bargain, with no ski tows or chairlifts to pay for. You are less likely to break a leg on X-C skis than in downhill skiing and if you have never been on skis before there's less to learn before you start enjoying yourself.

### NORDIC SKI EQUIPMENT

X-C skis, boots and bindings (the device which links the front of your boot to the ski) can be bought in good ski stores for children from the age of three upwards. A shop specializing in Nordic ski equipment and advertising in the kind of magazine read by ramblers, hill walkers and climbers, could be your best bet. Such a shop may send you goods on approval. It's worth asking. And when you do, send any measurements which might help.

*X-C Skis* The most important decision you have to make at first is the kind of ski you will buy. It helps if you can try on various skis of differing widths and patterns before choosing. If your local outdoor shop doesn't sell skis, they may still be able to give you the name of an X-C ski enthusiast who lives near you and might help. There might even be an X-C ski club in the area. Ski touring areas like Aviemore in the Highlands will let you try out several kinds of ski if you're renting. Then you can decide more easily yourself.

Why is it so important to get it right? The reason that X-C skis don't slip back when you climb up snow slopes is that a length of the underside of the ski below and to either side of your foot grips the snow like chewing gum sticking to a carpet. This part of the ski is known as the 'kicking strip'.

When you stand on the ski your body weight presses it down, squashing it flat on to the snow. As it sticks, you kick forward your other ski – momentarily unweighted and therefore free to slide. This is further helped because X-C skis are slightly cambered – or arched – from tip to tail. When you take your weight off the centre of the ski it springs back up off the snow a fraction like a steel spring.

The question you have to ask is what kind of kicking strip do you want? There are two kinds of ski. One has a smooth-bottomed kicking strip which you rub with a special wax that sticks to the snow when you force the ski down with your body weight. The kind of wax used depends on the snow conditions and temperature at the time. The other kind of kicking strip is made of a design that will grip the snow without wax. A popular one, for example, consists of scores of tiny plastic fish scales. They let you slide forward but prevent you slipping back.

Your choice will depend very much on where you live and the type of person you are. If you live in the south of England where snow may be limited and your skiing possibly restricted to just a few outings each winter, then the convenience of a waxless ski could be the thing. If you live in North Wales, the Derbyshire Peak District, the Yorkshire Dales, the Lake District or in much of Scotland where snow tends to remain a long time on high ground you may prefer a waxable ski.

However, if you are quickly bored with technical details such as testing snow conditions before you apply what you hope is the correct wax, go for a waxless ski. Although modern waxing technique is easy, it is also easy to make mistakes if you don't know what you're doing.

It must be pointed out, though, that the waxless ski does not perform as well as a waxable ski correctly treated. Waxless skis are in comparison a bit draggy and 'wooden'. You have to use more effort to push them forward. They can also backslip a little on hills, which means you sweat more to reach the crest.

Three final points: buy a ski with metal edges if you intend skiing mountains and moors; avoid a long waxless kicking strip if you weigh little (it won't slide easily downhill); choose a ski that reaches the palm of your hand as you stand with hand raised above head.

*X-C Ski Boots*   Light touring boots look like smart training shoes cut low at the ankle. For the heavier kind of X-C skis used on mountains you need footwear that resembles a light hiking boot with a moulded rubber sole as worn by hill walkers and climbers, in case conditions become too bad for skiing and you have to walk.

The welts of X-C ski footwear stick out beyond the toes in a square shape. They look as if the factory has forgotten to trim off waste material at the toe of the boot.

*Ski Bindings*   The three-pin binding is very simple and effective. You press the toe of your boot down on top of three tiny pegs sticking upright from the binding plate. These coincide with three small holes under the square part of the front of the boot. Your foot now fits in the correct position on the ski.

Snap the toe clip down on top of the square part of the welt which protrudes beyond the toes. You are now ready to ski, the heel lifting high whenever you walk.

*Ski Poles*   An aluminium-shafted pole will bend but won't break. It needs a 'butterfly basket' which prevents the pole sinking too deep when you stab it into the snow. The pole which reaches your armpit as you stand upright is the correct length one for you.

*Ski Waxes*   There are fourteen waxes, colour-coded for different snow conditions. Confusing? Not when you use a modern two-wax system: one kind of wax is for below-freezing temperatures, the other for above-freezing when the snow is wet. You apply the wax with a piece of cork or polystyrene and a hot waxing iron. You remove old wax quickly with a scraper, liquid wax remover and a rag. The instructions on the wax packet tell you all you need to know.

*Roller-skis* This is the way enthusiasts train but it is expensive. However, there may be a roller-ski or X-C ski club in your area where you can have a go. You stand on short metal bars with rubber rollers at each end and pole yourself across empty car parks and along quiet roads. The rollers are fitted with bindings for X-C boots. They also have a ratchet device to prevent them slipping back as you climb uphill and allow you to kick yourself forward.

LEARNING TO SKI CROSS-COUNTRY

The snow in your local park or field is a good place to begin. Carefully slide around in a loop to leave a large oval of twin ski tracks. Then try gliding around and around the same tracks without skis to get the feel of things.

If you fall, get up by crawling forward on your hands and knees, rising to your knees and getting up. Dust yourself down and start over again.

*X-C skiing*                                     *Two-phase Nordic technique*

Pick up the poles, slip your hands through the straps and try bending your knees more as you stride. As you step forward with one foot, plant the pole in the *opposite* hand in front of you and push off with both ski and pole. You'll start gliding. When you lose momentum, do the same thing with the other foot and pole. (Right foot, left pole and vice versa.)

This is the basic step, called the 'two-phase'. At first you may tend to tip over and fall, but as your balance becomes surer you'll find yourself gliding several metres forward with each step.

Try some slight uphill inclines too. It will be necessary to shorten your steps because you won't be able to glide. Then when you move downhill on the other side of the incline, you'll naturally take longer strides, and finally just push off occasionally with both poles to maintain your speed. This is called 'double poling'.

Take a short trip around the park. You'll feel clumsy, just as skaters do for the first time. But soon you'll notice you're gliding, even skating (this is the basis of the 'step turn' which is easy to learn if you've ever roller-skated) around corners and down gradients. As you grow more comfortable you'll waste less effort. Each time you take a step, push off with your ski and propel yourself with your pole. In what seems like no time at all you'll have joined the ranks of Nordic skiers!

## CYCLO-CROSS BICYCLE RIDING

Balancing a bicycle over mountains and moors, on disused coal tips and waste ground, and through peat bogs and rivers . . . that's cyclo-cross. Popular in Europe and Scandinavia, it is also becoming increasingly so in the United States. There they call it *mountain riding* or *desert riding*.

British cyclo-cross fills a sporting calendar where races feature on many weekends of the year. As many as six or more cyclo-cross events may take place on a particular Saturday or Sunday in different venues throughout the

United Kingdom. But this high sporting activity can also be used as one of the great outdoor adventure pursuits too.

Using a bicycle cyclo-cross style will allow you to follow in the tracks of hill walkers and backpackers at your own speed, and with one advantage over them. You cover the ridable stretches of terrain faster – even though this is partly offset because you have to carry your bike at times – so you can complete a longer route in the same time. Bridleways, footpaths, country lanes, forest trails and any common land can be ridden at will. Some cyclists even go pass-storming over the high passes of Snowdonia, Lakeland and the Highlands.

PREPARING YOUR BIKE

Any bike will do apart from BMXs. This is ironic because the BMX is *the* bike for stunting on rough ground. However, it is too heavy for cyclo-cross. Otherwise any straight or drop-handlebar cycle will be fine. Even ordinary tyres are all right at first, though later you will want to opt for proper studded ones.

You need very little preparation. Mudguards should be removed, handlebars need taping well and brake blocks must not be set too close to the wheel rims so that mud, leaves and so on can pass through the narrow gap.

Set the position of the saddle as far back as it will go. This will keep your weight over the back wheel where it's needed on soft ground.

Ask a cycle shop to change the block (the gearing sprockets on the back wheel) so there are twenty-seven teeth on the big cog which is your lowest gear and fourteen on the smallest cog for top. This, according to experts, will let you ride up the side of a house!

Fit a handlebar gear control lever. You insert this into one of the open ends of the handlebars to give you finger tip control during moments when both hands must be kept on the handlebars and yet you need to change gear.

Toe clips help when you most need the power. If you take

a pair of old soccer or rugby boots and slice off the studs under the front half – leaving say half a dozen studs at the rear of the shoe – you can slip the toes into the toe clips as you step on the pedals.

You will need to carry your cycle uphill and over unridable sections. If you are right-handed, sling the frame over your right shoulder, leaving your hands free to hold the bike wherever it feels most comfortable for you. To make it more comfortable where the frame meets the shoulder, roll up tightly a strip of foam rubber or the kind of plastic used for campers' insulating tent pads and tape it firmly into the angle of the frame where the crossbar meets the tube coming down from below the saddle. It will make a terrific difference on the sections where you have to leg it, lugging your bike.

After each cyclo-cross session, clean your bike by dousing it in a stream or with buckets of water. To prevent rust, squirt plenty of WD-40 aerosol spray on to all the moving parts. Thin lubricating oil is not as good; it picks up tiny particles of grit and leads to unnecessary wear.

### HINTS AND TIPS ON CYCLO-CROSS RIDING

. There is no need to enter cyclo-cross events such as The Three Peaks Cyclo-Cross Race, where three mountains in the Yorkshire Dales are cycled over punishing terrain. You can go off with friends and cycle many mountains and moors via the tracks and footpaths used by hill walkers and climbers, and all in your own good time.

Having said this, if cyclo-cross racing does appeal there is ample opportunity. At many cyclo-cross events there are schoolboy races. And when there is the demand, schoolgirls are not left out either.

Whichever way you decide to learn, here are some riding (and walking!) techniques that the experts use. They will certainly help on any cyclo-cross trips you take into the great outdoors.

Carrying your bicycle uphill or down, the frame is slung over one shoulder. On steep slopes you will find the front

*Carrying a cyclo-cross bike*

wheel tends to foul the ground rearing up in front of you, so turn the bike around and replace it on your shoulder with the rear wheel forward and the front wheel hanging down behind you. The foam rubber or plastic padding still fits on to your shoulder but because the back wheel is tilted high in this position, the bicycle no longer touches the ground.

Going over a stile, and carrying the bike the conventional way with handlebars forward, bend from the hips so that the bicycle pivots to clear the top of the stile supports which otherwise tend to catch the back wheel as you descend on the other side.

Swing – or kissing – gates are no problem if you just walk through holding the bike high, both hands grasping the frame.

You can even vault a locked five-barred gate. Lifting the bicycle over the top, lower it down and lean it against the far side of the wall with the frame and rear wheel propped against the gate. Now, gripping the top of the gate with one hand and, leaning down, the crossbar with your other, do a push-up on the arms and roll your body and both legs together over the top of the gate like a pole vaulter clearing the bar.

When riding, remember to sit well back in the saddle. This is preferable to standing on the pedals because it forces the back wheel down to get a better grip on the ground.

Watch the ground like a hawk. Terrain changes all the time. Going from grass to greasy rock, for example, means if you are going to brake it had better be before the slick rock is reached and not on top of it.

Shale is like loose ball bearings; be ready *before* your tyres actually connect and your bicycle begins to act up.

Cattlegrids, slippery with a layer of rubber from passing tyres, are particularly nasty. You can come off unless both wheels are lined up straight before your wheels come in contact with the metal bars. You should also brake before the grid rather than directly on it.

On a really bumpy stretch of open countryside it is better to pedal too fast than too slow. The slower you progress the more your tyres will follow every contour in the surface of the ground. At speed it is quite different. You 'ride' over the bumps and skim along their tops so long as you keep watching ahead for really serious obstacles and weave a path that is more or less continuously 'rough' in the same way.

Potholes along the track of your wheels can be smoothed out in this way so long as they are not too wide and sheer-sided. When, however, broad ditches and gaps such as drainage channels cross your path you can jump them. The leaping technique is best practised on a grassy patch with softer landings. As you approach the gap in the ground, sit back on the saddle and lift the front wheel just before taking off. Clear the hole as if doing a wheelie, letting your weight go forward as the front wheel touches down on the far side so that the rear wheel now rises and – unweighted – follows its example. It takes time to perfect this, and timing is the problem. At first you tend to throw your weight too far forward as the front wheel touches down on the far side of the gap. Result: you are sent over the handlebars. But judge it just right, as comes with practice, and you begin to do it out in the wilds without even thinking.

## THE POSSIBILITIES OF CYCLO-CROSS

Besides races, cyclo-cross events also feature 'reliability trials'. These are a twenty-five-mile rugged ride, say, over the roughest country. It's not so much who comes first – just completing the arduous route is the aim for everybody taking part.

Using this principle, cyclo-cross can take you anywhere walkers go and in many cases more easily and a good deal swifter. The choice of lovely routes on peaks and moors, downs and fens, along coastlines and river or canal banks is endless.

A day sack on your back packed lightly with food, spare sweater, waterproofs and so on, with a waist belt attached to prevent it swinging about, is all you need, though if you plan bivouacking a couple of nights out in wilderness country a saddlebag and carrier over the rear wheel is best. The whole idea of cyclo-cross touring is to feel free and without restriction of any sort. You have enough on your plate carrying the bike . . .

# 5

## Hill Walking, Scrambling and Gorge Walking

No other outdoor activity offers the same rewards for so relatively little cost as hill walking. It requires only the most basic equipment and no training. Hill walking is a fine activity for teaching yourself from scratch as you go with friends.

Getting to the hills can prove expensive, but it helps to share the cost of travelling by car with friends.

High ground is lonely and wild, rugged and inhospitable. It calls for the same consideration and care a cragface demands of a rock climber or the air currents created by a hill slope require from a hang glider pilot. In some respects the way of the hill walker can be equally as dangerous.

### THE HAZARDS OF MOUNTAIN WEATHER

Anybody caught in mountain weather at its worst will find it difficult to think, let alone navigate and preserve body heat. That is how serious conditions can become high on the hill while towns and villages below enjoy a mild day.

It is colder on the tops than in the valleys for two reasons: air temperature drops by about 4°F in every 1,000 ft, and the chilling effect of the wind has to be experienced to be believed. With the added likelihood that your clothing is damp from the elements or from your own perspiration, and the wind cuts through it non-stop, the only safe thing to do in conditions like these is go down quickly.

British hills are only modestly high compared with other mountain ranges. Yet they are surrounded by three of the world's most tempestuous seas and consequently are subject to fast-contrasting weather variations with little or no warning. A beautifully crisp day often develops into a raging blizzard on Scottish hills in particular, and this can happen within the space of half an hour due to a change of wind direction.

By no means everyone is sufficiently interested in weather to read up about it. The least anyone can do before starting out for a day on the hills, however, is pick up a telephone and dial the daily weather report number.

## HOW TO KEEP ON TOP OF HILL WALKING

If you watch a moorland shepherd at work you will see the difference between ordinary cross-country rambling and hill walking. He may be tiring at the end of his day, but he strides forward, balanced, with his arms slightly outstretched and seeming to float on air. For hours on end his movement is apparently effortless. How do you pick up this skill?

To walk like a human hovercraft, try this at home. Stand with your back to a wall with your chin up and your feet about 7–8 cm apart. Don't look down but sway forwards as if pivoting from the ankles. At the split second before you lose your balance, you will be obliged to rise up on your toes and stride forward, pushing off first with the ball of your foot (it doesn't matter which one) and then with your big toe. The other foot strikes the ground first and becomes the pusher for your next stride. By continuing to lean forward a little and swinging the arms in a rather exaggerated way to start with, you will put your own gravity-pull and momentum to work and start to enjoy the rhythms of an accomplished hill walker.

The thing is not to overdo it and try to go too quickly at first. This is very hard to do. The natural inclination is to speed up from the start. Reduce your speed when you feel the least bit tired or hot or, worse, a little wet and cold.

With practice, and I mean after walking up one or two easy mountains, you will be able to distinguish between a shakedown and a cruising speed. Later on you should be able to slip into an overdrive gear like that on a powerful car. Instead of making hard work of the walking, you will glide along.

## GOING UPHILL AND COMING DOWN

The steepening gradient of a mountainside makes all the difference between walking on the level and climbing. Does this sound obvious? You would be surprised how many people don't realize and fail to adapt their walking style because of it.

The particular kind of step forward just described depends on the flat of your foot being placed on the ground and not just the ball of the foot. To walk uphill in any other way is to resist nature and the fatigue in your legs and body will quickly prove this.

Nature works like this. While the angle of the ground is easy you walk with both feet pointing forward. Things a little steeper? Then both feet begin to splay outwards naturally. A further increase of the angle and both body and feet will begin to turn sideways so that you walk uphill in zigzags. Occasionally you may need to press a hand on the slope to keep in balance.

If the slope continues to steepen, you will find one foot naturally begins to point across the slope while the other points back downhill. Steeper still, and both feet will turn to point back downhill while you continue climbing upwards in a diagonal direction and going backwards.

Throughout this natural sequence of events, the feet remain flat on the slope. You will feel all the fresher so long as you keep the pace slow.

If it becomes impossible to zigzag up the steep part, you will need to tackle it head-on by turning sideways to the slope but going directly uphill one foot at a time like someone carrying heavy furniture upstairs.

Coming downhill, different stresses act on the body. The heart and lungs no longer labour, and everything seems to concentrate on the legs which act as shock-absorbers. You should keep them slightly bent when possible. Again, the important thing is to feel comfortable. On steep yielding ground, however, it is preferable to stiffen the legs and drive the heels in. This goose-step gives a better purchase on the ground as you make each stride.

Watch the ground ahead rather than chatting to friends on the descent. Unfortunately people who have not done this have sometimes gone head over heels while turning around in the middle of saying something to the person just behind.

Aim for any level places on the ground ahead where you can exert a braking force if you feel your legs beginning to run away with you. Take short steps. Turn sideways. And remember the key rule of descent: *lean forward as you come downhill.*

You will not topple face forwards as you fear so long as you keep pace with your feet. Your body will remain in balance, precarious though it feels at first, and will press the soles of your feet against the slope in the very best position of all to gain the most grip.

## SECRETS OF MOUNTAIN NAVIGATION

The most common reason for a rescue call-out on the hills is faulty navigation. This can only be guarded against by practising map reading and compass work on safe, low-lying ground and in bad visibility – in the dusk, say, or even later with the help of your head torch. It is too late to start when the mist comes down. Unfortunately that is the usual mistake – not starting to navigate until it is too late. By then the exact location of the group isn't known. It is doubly important to make it a habit to navigate all the time on mountains. The weather may be brilliantly sunny with fantastic views, but you should still keep tabs on your rate of progress.

It all boils down to being interested. And it starts from planning your route in the comfort of your home. Should the weather then turn nasty, you will be in a much better position to help yourself.

ROUTE PLANNING OVER HILLS

In hill country there is a lack of landmarks to help pinpoint your position. No windmills or church spires are likely to loom up on the horizon.

However, there are certain natural features which will help you identify your position, such as lakes (their distinctive shapes help); streams (unfortunately these are not always reliable as in summer they can dry up and in winter be covered by snow); trees (the higher you climb, the easier it is to check the shape of plantations on the slopes below, but forest boundaries can change shape in a surprisingly short time); mountain paths (paths offer the easiest way in hills and are cairned with heaps of stones at intervals as a result, but you cannot always trust them on paper as map-makers have been known to get them wrong); and crags (the hachures on maps which show crags, and which are drawn to scale, are of the utmost importance because you should steer clear of them when planning your route).

The features which have most bearing on your route, however, are contours. They are the ground you will be walking over. They will determine whether your day is exhilarating or simply exhausting. The principles behind choosing a good mountain route are easy to remember. Select a backbone of high ground so that once you have reached a height you will keep it. Go up the steeper end of such a stretch of mountain crest and come down the less steep end (thereby avoiding crags and waterfalls coursing down into the valley below) rather than the other way round. It doesn't matter if there are individual summits along your chosen route. Having gained height early in the day, you have broken the back of the climbing. The ups and downs of skyline tops will prove nowhere near as taxing as the first long haul out of the valley to get you up high.

All that remains is for you to keep on course, always knowing where you are and checking your rate of progress on your route card.

THE ROUTE CARD

Draw a series of columns down a piece of stiff cardboard you can tuck into your map case. Head them thus:

| From To | Direction | Distance | Height climbed | Time | Remarks |
|---------|-----------|----------|----------------|------|---------|
|         |           |          |                |      |         |

You now have a frame of reference on which to plan a mountain walk in advance, keeping a margin of safety you would never have had otherwise.

Begin by breaking up your route into easily digestible chunks and string them one after the other down the *From–To* column. For example, a trip of twelve miles might be split into half a dozen or more stages.

Let us miss out the *Direction* column just now and go on to the next one for *Distance*.

The distance you walk is shown by the map's scale. This can be measured either with a piece of string or by ticking off the straights and bends along the edge of a piece of card. Translate the distance you decide is covered on the map into kilometres or miles and enter them in the *Distance* column.

*Height climbed* is jotted down in its column, ignoring any height you drop down from individual summits along the skyline and your final descent into the valley at the conclusion of your day. Tot this up by adding the distance between the contours you will be covering. If you first climb a peak 2,800 ft high, then descend 500 ft and then ascend another summit which tops 3,010 ft the height climbed to that point would be: 2,800 plus the 500 ft lost and then retrieved, plus another 210, totalling 3,510 ft.

Calculate the time you will take by a rule of thumb formula, and enter this in the *Time* column. The formula does not take into account rest periods, the wind against you or the fact that your party may not be firing on all cylinders. However, it is a better estimate than nothing. You can choose whether to work in kilometres or miles. The first formula measures distance in metric and height in imperial. According to this you walk at 4 km an hour and add two minutes for every 50-ft contour line (which is the same as saying you can expect to climb 1,500 ft in an hour). According to the other formula you walk at 3 miles an hour and add an hour for every 1,500 ft climbed.

And the column for *Remarks*? Enter warnings of crags and other obstacles to avoid.

This brings us back to the missing *Direction* column. In order to complete it we must first look more closely at how to read a compass correctly.

## HOW TO ORIENTATE YOURSELF WITH COMPASS BEARINGS

It helps enormously if, whenever you look at a map, you can visualize direction according to number of degrees, for instance 360°, 180°, 90° and 270° for North, South, East or West. Numbers are the language of the Silva or Suunto compasses I recommended in Chapter 2. By using one of these instruments you can write down on your route card the direction to take in case you meet mist or darkness along the way. You note down this direction in numbers rather than words.

Diagram 6 shows the sequence of things to do. Having first acquainted yourself with the parts of the compass labelled here, make a bet with yourself as to the number of degrees the bearing might be. (In this case it will obviously be a figure somewhere between South and West or, as we will estimate, 180° and 270°.) This is a double-check. It prevents serious mistakes should you accidentally place the compass the wrong way around when working out the bearing from the map.

Next place the edge of the compass along both A and B as if ruling a line between the two. Is the Direction of Travel (DOT) arrow pointing the way you want to go? *Then do not move the compass baseplate from now on.*

As the diagram shows, you turn the compass housing

around until the red orientating lines are parallel with the N–S grid lines on the map. The North orientating line now points to the top of the map.

Now take the compass from the map. Read the bearing where the DOT arrow touches the dial. Check with your original bet. As this is a grid bearing, convert it into a working bearing (or magnetic bearing) by adding whatever the number of degrees your map advises you should, either in its margin or among its key.

And magnetic variation? The Magnetic North Pole moves about inside the Arctic Circle and deflects the compass needle, depending whereabouts you are, to the West or East, so you must adjust a certain number of degrees to compensate for it. In Lake District mountains, for example, you simply twist the dial to add a further 8° as I write this.

Finally, to discover the way you should walk, hold the compass in the palm of your hand and turn *yourself* and the compass around until the red end of the magnetic needle hovers on top of the North orientating line. The DOT arrow now points the way (not the red end of the magnetic needle).

HOW TO WALK ON A COMPASS BEARING

There is a risk that walking on a compass bearing can lead you further astray than ever. This happens if you talk to friends and let your concentration wander. The wind can also help by pushing you to one side without your realizing it, so that although you are walking in the correct direction you keep stepping further and further to one side.

Fix your eyes on something ahead on the line of the bearing. Put your compass away and walk to this point, repeating the technique when you arrive. The 'something' can be a rock or clump of reeds or, better still, another person. By lining up two people on a bearing you can arrive at a more accurate reckoning. You walk to the nearest person, once satisfied they are standing along the track of the bearing. Then, consulting the compass once more, you send them on ahead again and repeat the process.

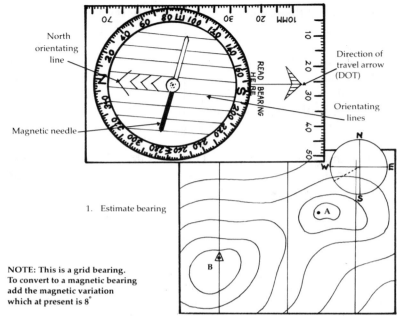

1. Estimate bearing

NOTE: This is a grid bearing.
To convert to a magnetic bearing
add the magnetic variation
which at present is 8°

*Lifting a compass bearing from the map*

If you reach a path, stick to it if the compass shows it leads in the right direction. In any event you should emerge from the mist several hundred metres below the summit.

The first thing you do on seeing the valley below is to consult the map and check it is the right valley! It is a common mistake to drop into the wrong valley because you have made a compass error on the skyline of as little as two or three degrees out. If you don't realize your mistake and correct it in time, you could add several weary hours to your walk as you make your way back on the wrong side of the mountain.

AVOIDING THE HAZARDS OF COMPASS BEARINGS

Jet fighter pilots use a moving map in the cockpit during their low-flying practice runs over mountains and moors. The map always depicts the ground below the right way up. Like a

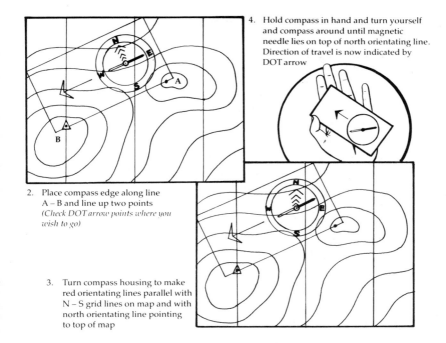

4. Hold compass in hand and turn yourself and compass around until magnetic needle lies on top of north orientating line. Direction of travel is now indicated by DOT arrow

2. Place compass edge along line A – B and line up two points *(Check DOT arrow points where you wish to go)*

3. Turn compass housing to make red orientating lines parallel with N – S grid lines on map and with north orientating line pointing to top of map

slice of lemon in a rotating glass of Coca Cola, it stays pointing in the same direction.

In case the moving map breaks down, the pilot also carries an Ordnance Survey map. Before flying he rules straight lines of his track through the sky across the paper, just as the hill walker first checks out bearings for the *Direction* column of the route card. If you were to walk along the pilot's bearings, you would find they bisect the most awesome territory – crags, lakes, rivers, forests and Ministry of Defence bombing, shelling and electronic warfare testing ranges. The reason is obvious. Straight lines are no respectors of terrain. They simply take the shortest distance between two points.

This is why the stages *From–To* on your route card should be kept short. If you allow for too much distance in between, the chances are your compass bearing from A to B might lead you through the kind of terrain Jaguar and Tornado pilots skim over! Supposing, however, there is no way around the crag that lies across your proposed route. Then you will have to go round it using two or three separate bearings in succession. By timing yourself on each 'leg' you will then know when it's time to stop and take a fresh bearing.

How you time yourself along each leg depends on the formula you decide to use for your route card. Let us suppose you favour the 3-mph formula for your walking speed. If one of the legs then measures a mile exactly and there is no height-gain involved, you can reckon that after twenty minutes' walking in mist on a compass bearing you should be able to stop and reset your compass to a fresh bearing.

Orienteers use this technique by knowing how many double-paces (count for one foot only) they take over 100 metres or 100 yards. For the time being, however, the wristwatch method is a perfectly good alternative if you have practised it previously in a field or park near your home.

When there are two or three bearings involved in completing a stage, you can use both the *Direction* and *Remarks* columns to enter both the different bearings *and* the times you estimate it will take to travel along each one.

GOOD MAP READING

Fold your map carefully so the region you are walking is centred in the plastic window of your map case. It pays to use the largest scale of map in popular use, as it will prove easier to read.

If it rains so that moisture dots the surface of the map case when you consult it, resist the temptation to take the map out and have a closer look at it. The paper will become damp and smear the inside of the plastic window once you put it back in. Instead, flex the map and its case in both hands to stretch the transparent plastic tight over the map. Instantly the map is seen more clearly.

Never walk on a compass bearing while talking to a friend at your side. He or she can nudge you to one side without either of you realizing it.

The easiest position in which to hold the compass as you walk on a bearing is in front of your navel. Unfortunately this brings it within a short distance of your belt buckle, wristwatch and – if worn around the neck and hanging down your front – camera light meter, and all these can exert a powerful deflecting effect on the magnetic needle.

## EXTRA HAZARDS OF MOUNTAIN HIGH GROUND

Be careful of winds which can bowl you over. Make your retreat from the hill early, waiting out the worst gusts by lying on the ground and crawling when necessary. Flooded mountain streams can sweep away and drown people who try to cross, so be prepared to walk several extra miles to reach a bridge rather than risk being knocked off your feet. Hard patches of steep hillside snow can linger and consequently pose a real danger out of season. Detour around them as you would a swollen hillside stream. Gullies are frequently the scene of accidents, so avoid all crags unless a well-marked and classic hill walk is described in guidebooks of the area as passing through such a hazard-laden defile. Scree also causes a number of accidents every year as inexperienced walkers try to run down it and, gathering speed, become out of control and unable to stop. Avoid the scree lying on open mountainsides until you are more experienced.

## WINTER HILL WALKING

Once snow begins to fall on the hill, the whole complexion of mountain walking changes dramatically. Unfrozen, the new snow on the ground makes for unpleasant walking and clings to the soles of the boots. It is the gradual process of snow thawing through the day then freezing hard at night that binds it into the perfect surface that climbers dream about, where it has all the plasticity of an easily moulded snowball.

SPECIALIST HILL WALKING EQUIPMENT

The kind of snow cover that yields crisply to boot soles or crampon points, yet remains as firm and perfect as the icing on a cake, calls for extra equipment.

*The Ice Axe*   Never be tempted to go out without an ice axe just because you happen to be among the hills, snow falls overnight and you want to take advantage of it before it melts. Seven times out of ten you probably will be all right without its support but on those other three occasions you might need it quite without warning. An ice axe is as necessary on snow-bound hills as a rope is to the rock climber or buoyancy aid to the canoeist. Hill walkers should choose an ice axe that grazes the ground when held in the hand, finger and thumb round the narrow part of the head and arm down by the side.

The diagram shows a hole through the head of the axe, and a sling of nylon tape threaded through. This forms a wrist loop which locks your hand to the axe handle when you need it most, using the pick part of the axe's head for support on steep hard-frozen snow. The loop also ensures that you and the axe do not part company should you fall and have to use it to prevent you sliding downhill at high speed.

There are many ice axes on the market, some with short handles and viciously-angled or drooped picks. A number resemble the martial axes of historic battles. Their purpose is quite different from the one you need. They are ice climbing tools and you need only consider buying from this end of the range when you are ready for climbing ice-coated rock at high angles and need an ice-stabbing instrument in each fist. An ice axe just short of walking stick length, with a gently curved pick, is all you require now.

*Crampons and Boots*   You do not need a pair of crampons at first on snow-bound hills.

They make life easier when snow cover is hard and are essential when the slopes are glazed with ice. However, they

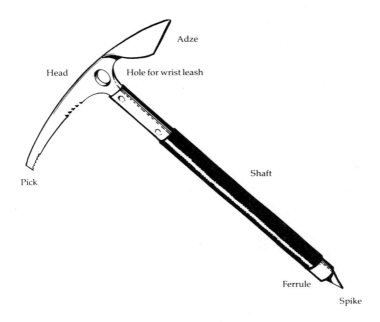

*Hill walking and general mountaineering ice axe*
(this is without wrist leash)

do need extra care. On soft snow, for example, they are a liability.

The most universally popular crampons are made by Salewa. They have twelve points and are articulated in the centre like a juggernaut lorry. You can fold them up doubled and store them inside a climbing helmet.

Crampons are only of any use when you have the proper boots. These must be rigid if you go ice climbing, but hill walkers can get away with a slightly less stiff boot such as the kind of heavy leather ones provided by many outdoor centres for the duration of each course.

The best boot is undoubtedly the plastic boot already recommended in Chapter 2. It looks like a ski boot but with a climbing-type moulded rubber sole underneath. These make both walking and climbing in winter feel incredibly secure and comfortable.

You should take your boots to the shop when you buy crampons, then they can be fitted together. The fit should be so snug that if you hold up a boot, the attached crampon will not drop off even when you knock the boot and even though the straps that attach crampon to boot when walking and climbing are unfastened. Do buy good crampon straps. The best ones are made from neoprene.

*Gaiters*   Gaiters are required to protect crampon points from accidentally snagging in the cloth of your pants. They should streamline the lower leg. Baggy gaiters are as dangerous as loose, flapping trousers when you wear crampons.

The combination of long thermal underpants, track suit bottoms and possibly over-trousers worn beneath your gaiters is businesslike. Climbing instructors remove the laces provided in the top of each gaiter for tying just below the knee. You need to lift the legs high when wearing crampons so the points don't accidentally snag on the hard-frozen slope, and this lace can catch on the crampon points when tied with bows.

Many inexperienced hill walkers make the mistake of wearing gaiters when there is no snow. This makes the legs unbearably warm.

WINTER HILL WALKING EXTRAS

It should go without saying that you take spare thin layers of clothing with you for winter hill walking. Also take extra food high in starch: honey sandwiches and sticky buns are great. You need a warm drink and the ideal is Complan in the flavour you favour. It is a complete meal in a drink. Extra warmth for the hands is best provided by thermal gloves (thin) and, if really cold, the climber's friend: Dachstein mitts. Don't forget spare head torch batteries and bulbs plus Elastoplast dressings, and lastly, spare socks in case (heaven forbid!) you anticipate traversing hills deep in soft snow.

USING THE ICE AXE

The most common form of injury on winter's mountains is a slip on steep snow or ice, and the inability to arrest one's fall immediately. To check this doesn't happen to you, always carry the axe in your hand when on mountains covered with snow. Don't leave it too late. Hill walkers and climbers who wait until they are in the middle of a steep slope to remove their axes from the loops on their rucksacks risk slipping before the only means of stopping themselves is at their disposal.

The safest measure is to practise on a really steep slope of hard-frozen snow at the beginning of each winter. The slope requires a safe basin of snow beneath so you can be sure of a soft landing.

Carry the ice axe as you would a walking stick. The pick should point to the rear with your hand on top.

Snow that collects in snowballs under your boots is too soft. You need well-refrigerated snow to practise. Let the weight of your boot and leg do the work. A swing of the leg should be enough to burst through the snow or at least to make a sufficiently-sized dent in it for you to be able to stand on it. This is preferable to kicking the slope to death with repeated bootings into the same place.

Climb in zigzags, the axe held by your inside hand (the one nearest to the snow). *This means every time you change direction your axe changes hands.* If the snow is too hard for the point at the bottom end of the handle to be inserted very far as you move upwards holding it like a walking stick, or if the incline is glazed with ice, grasp the ice axe across your body instead. *Again the hand nearest the slope holds the axe head, pick pointing down and ready to stab deep into the slope at a moment's notice.*

Let us imagine you are kicking steps uphill with your ice axe held in the walking stick position. You suddenly slip. What happens next should be reflex. Quickly grip the lower end of the axe handle with your other hand. As you begin to slide, roll over on to your front and *towards the same side as the head of your axe.* You are now in a position to press the weight of your chest down on top of the ice axe handle so its gently curved pick is driven into the slope like a dagger.

It does require practice. You should also try to self-arrest from a number of positions. Try being pushed bodily down the slope from an upside-down position as you lie on the snow with the axe head across your body in the pre-braking position. And wear cagoule and over-trousers. The slipperiness of the nylon will speed you faster down the steep snow.

CUTTING STEPS AND WALKING ON CRAMPONS

Icy slopes which resist your attempts to kick footholds can be climbed by slashing footholds with either the pick of your axe or a corner of the adze, and sometimes both. With training, one 'pull' will often be enough to fashion a foothold. You can manage such slopes much more easily, however, if you wear crampons. Try walking in them on gentle slopes at first. You will quickly find you need to lift the legs high so the points don't catch the surface of the ground in mid-step.

The two front 'cowcatcher' points of a twelve-point crampon will allow you to climb any slope direct, so long as you reach high and drive the axe pick into the hard snow above you every small step or two you take upwards. And keep one hand over the axe head and the other lower down the handle. For zigzagging or traversing, the remaining ten points of each crampon should be pressed flat-footed on the ground as we have already discussed in basic hill walking.

If the snow is so soft that snowballs collect under the crampons, you have two courses of action. Jettison the snowballs by tapping the boots every few paces with the handle of your ice axe or, better still, remove the crampons until you find hard snow on which to practise.

The self-arrest must also be perfected wearing your crampons. *This means keeping the knees bent and feet high so the points do not foul the slope in mid-flight.* The risk is that if they do catch they can send you somersaulting hopelessly out of control and unable to use your axe properly to stop in time.

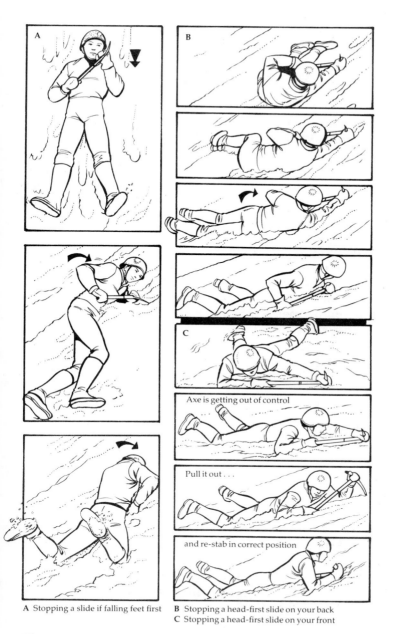

Axe is getting out of control

Pull it out . . .

and re-stab in correct position

A  Stopping a slide if falling feet first

B  Stopping a head-first slide on your back
C  Stopping a head-first slide on your front

*Three ways of ice-axe self arrest*

SNOW BOMBS

Avalanche conditions cause a number of accidents in Scotland each year. They can also occur in England and Wales with the same result. It is important that hill walkers as well as climbers study snow structure on the day they actually set out.

The best way to do this is to dig a pit and assess the strength of the layers of old snow under the surface. These form whenever snow lies on the surface for some time. When more snow falls it makes a separate layer. As you dig through these layers they become as obvious as ring markings in a tree.

Collapsing cornices where the snow is wet are a real danger. Formed by wind blowing from the skyline out over space and gradually building up into solid masses overhanging slopes below, cornices can either dump tons of snow on top of you if you happen to be directly underneath, or collapse if you are foolish enough to step on top of them. The answer is to keep well back from the edge of any summit plateau or skyline crest thickly plastered with snow.

RISKS OF OVERNIGHT STRANDING

For four months each year British days are very short. It is much better to start in darkness than to finish the day battling with spindrift and the merciless wind when reserves of strength are ebbing at just the very time when you need them most.

## MOUNTAIN SCRAMBLING

Hill walking routes which require you to use hands as well as feet for certain stretches of skyline crest are tremendously popular. They offer a taste of 'real' climbing and as such should be treated with respect. They are in effect rock climbs not quite serious enough to need a rope.

Before ascending a rock climb, climbers consult the guidebook. This gives details of the cragface up which they hope to climb: height, standard of difficulty and notes on specific problems. You should do the same when planning a mountain scrambling trip. There are a number of hill walking guide-books which analyse popular skyline scrambles.

Doing your homework pays dividends. It forewarns you of any 'Bad Steps'. These involve certain places poised high above space which need extra care. An example would be to attempt to climb direct from England's highest mountain, Scafell Pike, on to the summit of neighbouring Scafell up a section of cliff called *Broad Stand*.

The guidebook will warn the inexperienced off such places. It is far safer to take the easier, if longer, detour around the danger-point and leave such spots until you are more experienced and more at home on mountains.

Choose only the Striding Edges for your early scrambles. *Striding Edge* is a skyline edge on Helvellyn in the Lake District. It has so many hand- and foot-holds and resting places on welcome platforms and ledges you would be hard put to fall. It is an easy, well-marked and highly popular trip.

Just to make sure you do keep in contact with the rock, here are the basic things you should keep in mind. Come back down and rest if a piece of rock climbing on your scramble is proving awkward. Test all your handholds before pulling on them by thumping the rock with a fist to see if anything moves slightly or sounds hollow. Step up on your feet rather than pulling up on your arms. Only move a foot upwards if the other foot and both hands are securely placed (and ditto the other limbs when it is their turn to move). Call 'Below!' if you disturb a rock to give due warning of the danger. Avoid all scrambling routes in winter unless you are prepared for ice climbing with the proper tools and rope.

## GORGE WALKING

Curiosity about the unknown is the chief attraction of gorge walking. You never know what awaits you round the next corner and there are many of those during a gorge walk.

Rock walls on either side dwarf you like the jaws of a mighty vice. You feel like a pigmy as you scramble up the bed of the water course in between. Some gorges, even in Britain, are so deep their innermost recesses see little sun.

Gorge walkers explore the most secret parts of hills. The gorges, canyons and ravines channelling the water that drains off summit slopes to the valley via waterfalls and cataracts offer a kind of sport only paralleled by caving. The difference with gorge walking is that you begin at the bottom and go up. You also gorge walk in broad daylight as there is no enclosing roof above. And, unlike caverns, gorges are not well documented in guidebooks.

Gorge walkers enter their chosen cleft in the hillside at the lowest point where the water emerges near the valley bottom. Then, like early cavers on pioneering explorations, they have to be prepared to take whatever the giant uphill passage ahead throws at them. At the top they have the choice of either descending into the valley via easy hillside slopes or continuing to the skyline above as a hill walk.

Because they offer such a highly adventurous route, gorge walks should be made at first in the company of an experienced climber or caver. However, four to six young people of equal ability and plenty of common sense should be able to complete a good gorge walk on their own.

The first thing to do is check your public library for those guidebooks that might help. Hill walking and winter climbing guides are sometimes valuable in this respect. Rock climbing guides might be more so. But the most help is any mountain scrambling guidebook that covers the region you want to visit.

No guidebook? Then the map can hint at certain things and tell you others.

It will tell you the height and length of the large ravines shown on mountain slopes. It will also suggest that any gorge cutting through a hillside of closely packed contours is likely to be over your head.

The closer the contours, the steeper the gradient. This could well mean big waterfalls inside the cleft, best avoided by giving that particular canyon a miss from the start.

So first you look for a ravine that lies up an easy-angled hillside and which is not above, say, 1,000 ft in height. This will give the most likely chance of small pools and canals and short, friendly cascades, and yet be sporting into the bargain.

The map will also show where the ravine forks. You will be well advised to take those branches that climb the mildest-angled slopes and end where the hillside is open and welcoming rather than vertical and craggy.

The next step is to telephone for a weather report. Heavy rain could trap you in an amazingly short time. The water level will rise so quickly that your only chance will be to wait on some ledge that you hope will remain out of harm's way.

The third thing you should do is to leave a note with a responsible person giving the name and map reference of your intended gorge walk.

Track suit, thermal underwear and training shoes or boots are the basic clothing you require. If you explore in bathing costumes in summer you still need to keep training shoes on the feet and wear a climbing or canoeing or caving helmet on the head.

Take reserve warm clothing and food in one or two day sacks which you can take turns carrying. Whistles and first-aid kit should be included too.

Non-swimmers should not go gorge walking without the kind of buoyancy aid worn by canoeists. These are more suitable than lifejackets which are designed to support an unconscious body in the water. They are bulky, and trying to rock climb up the short steps of your gorge is made more difficult by wearing them. The buoyancy aid, by contrast, is a kind of slim-line vest padded with plastic foam. It is comfortable and provides good insulation too. If in any doubt about any members of your group, pack one into a day sack just in case it's needed.

If you begin to meet up with seriously steep and high waterfalls and rock steps festooned in slippery damp moss, it would be best to turn back. You will find plenty of other options on the map which could prove much more your style and a lot less risk-laden.

There is one more piece of good advice. Cavers and potholers frequently plunge into deep water and barge their way through to save time. A gorge walk should be treated differently. Here it pays to look on your outing as *climbing*. Pools and canal-like stretches of water should be traversed by your climbing across one or other of the rock walls on either side just above the surface of the water. This way is not just safer. In your efforts to keep dry, it teaches you a great deal about the principles of rock climbing.

# 6

## *Bivouacking, Camping and Snow-Holing*

In some ways sleeping out is basically the same whether on a National Express coach or in a mountain hut. Details which are important for your comfort and well-being tend to be learned the hard way – through experience. This is why sleeping out first on your lawn or in a neighbouring field is so valuable.

For example, if sleeping on a coach curl up with your knees against the back of your own seats (if you are lucky enough to have two seats spare to yourself) rather than the other way around if you want to be comfortable. And in a mountain hut, wrap more blankets around the bunk mattress than you place around yourself or put plenty of blankets under your sleeping bag.

## LIGHTWEIGHT CAMPING KIT

You need only the most basic camping equipment. This will look like a lot of extra expense on top of everything else, even so. Remember, then, that much is shared if you go with friends.

A way to cut down cost is to pick and choose. Pick the smaller items you need from inexpensive stores like Army & Navy, but choose the tent, sleeping bag, insulating pad and cooker from a good specialist outdoor shop.

SLEEPING BAG

This is the first item you should buy because then you can sleep out needing little else.

The best sleeping bags are those which trap air inside their goose or duck down filling. Although costly, these are very light, very warm and can be squashed into a space that looks like next to nothing. A popular alternative is a range of synthetic fillings like Hollofil, Thermalon, Fibrefil2 and P3. These are bulkier than down and not as long-lasting, but they are cheaper and unaffected by moisture. Wring them out when wet and you can still keep warm inside.

Buy the best bag you can afford. The most expensive bags, however, are unnecessary unless you intend camping all year round.

INSULATING PAD

Buy a closed-cell plastic foam pad such as a Karimat or Bergmat. It can be carried unprotected outside rucksack or bike, rolled up tight and held together by thick rubber bands. Pads cost little, are as light as a feather and nowadays are used by Laplanders instead of their traditional reindeer skins because they are so convenient and comfortable!

STOVE AND COOKING UTENSILS

Cookers running on camping gas, petrol, paraffin and solid fuel have their advantages, but I recommend the meths storm cooker made by Trangia, Optimus or Fjallraven. They live up to their name (you can cook in the wind), are safe and you buy a set of pots with them, everything nesting together as a unit. They are also very stable as they have a potstand which surrounds both the pot on the boil and the burner below.

Whatever kind of stove you use, you also need a plastic mug, an eating bowl (not aluminium as it gets too hot), a cheap cutlery set, a roll-up plastic water bag and a baby can opener.

TENT

Buy a double-skinned tent rather than a single-skinner. The single-skin tent may look simpler and come out cheaper, but it will drip condensation on you in the night unless you are very careful.

A double-skinned tent works like this: first you pitch the nylon outer skin (or flysheet) which is designed to keep the rain and wind out; then you hang an inner tent inside the fly sheet. The inner tent is attached to the ground sheet which can then be pegged to the ground and the tent is ready to live in.

As the inner tent is made from breathable material, it allows the water vapour from your body to pass out rather than to condense on the inside of its walls, so you keep dry.

Your lightweight tent shouldn't weigh more than four or five pounds. It should have a bell end to give rainy weather cooking space as you lie in your sleeping bag inside. And there should be two tent poles at this end of the tent, braced together and forming an 'A' so that, looking out from inside, it would appear you are inside a pole-less tent – the 'A' of the poles straddling it.

If you find a good quality tent too costly, then buy a cheap two-skinned tent made in Japan or Taiwan and sold in High Street shops like Peters or Millets. Snags: groundsheets may soon need replacing and materials will not be as robust nor as well designed as with a tent made by, say, Ultimate, Vango, Robert Saunders, Fjallraven, Blacks or Bukta.

Should you be given a one-skin tent, sleep with the door open and try not to rub against the walls. Store wet clothing in a polythene bag and carry a big sponge for mopping condensation from the tent's insides.

As to the best size of tent – choose the two-man version if you're not sure.

## BIVOUACKING

Outward Bound students expecting a warm bed on their arrival in school often find themselves spending the night out on a mountainside – even though most of them can't tell one end of a mountain tent from another! Their bivvies consist of a sleeping bag, a survival bag, an insulating pad and a nightcap of Trangia-cooker-brewed tea and biscuits. That's bivouacking. It enables you to spend a night outdoors with few resources.

You can spend a similar night with virtually no preparation on your lawn, a friend's lawn, a nearby field or anywhere else that's convenient and safe.

Unroll your insulating pad on the ground, pressing it flat by kneeling on it and securing it by spreading a sheet of heavy-gauge polythene on top (bought from a garden centre or plastics warehouse). This 'groundsheet' can be kept down by tying a pebble into each folded-over corner with a piece of string. The string should be long enough to allow its other end to be wrapped around a heavy rock which then serves as an anchor – one at each corner. As a freshly unrolled insulating pad has a life of its own, this plastic groundsheet will help to flatten it out and keep it in one place until you lie down on top of it.

Unroll your sleeping bag, then unfold your survival bag and place the one inside the other. Your bivouac is now ready for you to wriggle inside. Once in the sleeping bag, you will be able to caterpillar it so far forward inside the heavy-duty polythene sleeve of the survival bag that there will be a considerable overlap at the end which will completely cover the top part of you, head and all.

It will reach over your head, I must add, without any risk of accidentally suffocating you. A proper survival bag is too thick to pose such a risk. And it will completely seal you from the cold and rain.

The last thing you should do lying deep inside your cocoon is to brew up some cocoa on the cooker. This can help sleep arrive that bit quicker. Then snuggle down into the sleeping bag, drawing the end of the survival bag well over your head and under your pillow of spare clothing or whatever.

In the morning, gloom. You will find that the water vapour from your body has been unable to pass through the plastic of the survival bag and has condensed on the inside like the steam from a kettle running down kitchen walls. (This is exactly what happens in a one-skin tent.) It will have made your sleeping bag damp on the outside. However, if you are using one of the synthetically-filled sleeping bags, as mentioned earlier in the chapter, it will still keep you warm. Both bags hung out to dry will do just that in a few hours.

## CAMPING

Backpacking or bikepacking, in either case you make your own way across the countryside carrying your home for the night. You are self-sufficient. To do this in comfort and with least wasted effort, here are one or two considerations to take into account.

### CHOOSING A RUCKSACK

The range of rucksacks available to you has never been wider. I much prefer the rucksack to the back frame, which is a large bag attached to a light rigid frame that you carry next to your back. The pack frame comes low down my list of equipment because the frame snags on trees, bushes, rocks and public transport. It catches the wind like a sail and can overbalance you without warning on high ground.

The rucksack you choose should be compatible with the outdoor activities you anticipate doing, and a climber's sack is ideal for most of the activities described in this book. This is shaped to your back and must be 'fitted' for you in a good outdoor shop. Its light internal flexible frame will help transfer some of the weight from shoulders to pelvis and hips. It is considerably larger than a day sack and so you will be able to fit into it all the kit you need for a weekend or longer camping out. Your day sack can still be carried inside your larger sack. Should you go rock climbing, for example from a camp site base, it comes into its own once more as you leave the larger sack behind.

BIKEPACKING

The first essential is that your bicycle is not too highly geared. Going uphill or against wind demands a low gear to avoid unnecessary effort. While with a sit-up-and-beg three-speed bike you know your limitations, owners of five- and ten-speed models could well have gear ratios that are too high. Ask a cycle shop to swap the block (the gearing sprockets) so that on a five-speed the rear sprockets have 13, 15, 17, 19 and 28 teeth and the chainwheel 32 teeth. And for a ten-speed, the rear sprockets should range from 14 to 34 teeth while the smaller inner chainwheel has 34 or 36 teeth and the other chainwheel 48.

One other extra is invaluable for girls, who have a wider pelvis: a Brooks B17 leather saddle.

Your other needs are few. Shoes can be training shoes or cycling shoes, though smooth soles are a disadvantage for walking. Clothing has to be thin and worn in layers. Cycle bags come in different arrangements. You might opt for two small panniers on the front wheel and two larger ones on the rear, or two small panniers on the front wheel plus a saddlebag, or a saddlebag and a handlebar bag.

Cycle bags should be supported by cycle bag carriers. These need to be strong and rigid. They should prevent the panniers moving when you pedal or corner sharply. They also prevent the saddlebag and handlebar bag from pressing on the tyres.

Maps, tools and a good cycle lock are your final necessities.

## WHERE TO GO

Plan only short day-trips at first, no more than five to seven miles across country on foot, or forty miles on your bicycle. Keep things flexible. If you spot an attractive camp site before reaching the one you planned and have second thoughts – why not? So long as you camp well before dark, fine.

Try to avoid arriving at your site too late. A farmer might refuse permission when you had counted on stopping at a certain place, or you might find a camp site full. The weather can always change, leaving you to pitch camp in gathering darkness and rain. So if a better 'pitch' takes your fancy en route, by all means consider it if nobody is expecting you somewhere further along your route that day.

## EQUIPMENT

Don't carry more than 20 lb. (and preferably 15 lb.) on your back for early backpacking excursions. As a good walking group number is four, each pair self-sufficient with their own two-man tent, much of the weight can be shared. Here's how.

### PERSONAL GEAR

Rucksack; insulating pad; sleeping bag; spare jumper and trousers; spare socks; waterproofs; gloves; scarf; hat; toilet gear; first-aid kit; torch and batteries; compass; map and whistle; mug; bowl, knife, fork, spoon.

### COMMUNAL KIT

Food; stove; tent; flysheet, inner tent, poles; two fuel bottles; candles; matches; roll-up water bottle.

FOOD

You will each need 2 lb. a day (say 5 lb. for a weekend). As an example of what you might take, breakfast, prepared lying in your sleeping bag inside the tent and cooking in the open doorway, could be porridge (soaked overnight and less likely to blow away than cornflakes), scrambled eggs (already prepared and stored in an airtight container), crispbread (it doesn't fall apart when damp like bread), marmalade and margarine (easy to spread). You would not need any lunch as such because you would eat sweets (candy), raisins, chocolate, flapjacks, Kendal mint cake and other energy-boosting foods throughout the day, though if you like a sandwich by all means take one or two.

A hot meal is welcome at night and boiling or stewing is easiest. Several ingredients can be cooked together in the same pot, and the hot water is recyclable for washing-up. Dried vegetables, mashed potato powder, dehydrated soups and curries are easy to cook and light to carry. Skip tins (liquid has to be drained off) except for tinned meat (for protein). Plastic-bagged meats and fish can be cooked in boiling water with the veg. Jams, meat pastes and condensed milk are all available in tubes.

Cheap supermarket packs can be broken into smaller portions before setting out.


PACKING

It's a good idea to line your rucksack either with a large plastic bag into which you put your gear so that it remains dry in the wettest weather (rucksacks are not 100 per cent waterproof), or with your insulating pad. (This is how rucksacks look so good in shop windows – they are lined with an insulating pad!)

First take your sleeping bag out of its stuff bag and push it down into the bottom of your lined rucksack. Putting a foot down inside on top of the sleeping bag helps to make room for the rest of your kit. Like dough in bread-making, it will rise again once your foot comes off, but keep in mind the pressure you need to apply and you will fit everything in!

Spare clothes can go next, then the rest. Keep the fuel tin away from the food, just in case. An extra safeguard is to line the screw-top of a fuel can with a fragment torn from a polythene bag. This will seal it perfectly.

The tent and waterproofs should be readily accessible at the top of the sack and under the top flap so that, if it is raining, you can pitch camp first without disturbing the rest of the sack (which you then unpack in the shelter of the tent).

With cycle bags, be careful not to overload the front panniers as this will affect the steering. The tent, insulating pad and sleeping bag can go on top of the carriers where only panniers on each side of the wheels are being used.

### ALL SYSTEMS GO!

Do you remember the most valuable points to make cross-country walking easier? Here's a quick re-run in case it helps.

A route card is always handy; a slow start is the ideal and the pace of the slowest member of your group should be your pace too; avoid high ground on early backpacking trips (over-ambition is the cause of many accidents); only wear water-proof 'shell' clothing when wet and windy and so avoid the 'heat-lag' caused by wearing too many clothes as your body's motor warms up; keep eating and drinking while you are on the move.

### PITCHING CAMP

Start and finish early both in summer and winter. In summer it will be pleasantly cool, in winter, there's more daylight for the early bird. On wet days stay inside your sleeping bag in your tent if you have no other plans.

When looking for your 'pitch' search for firm, level, dry turf in the lee of a wall, hedge, boulder or dip in the ground.

Avoid trees which bomb tents with sticky deposits. And before you put your tent up, roll on the ground. If it isn't comfortable, find somewhere else.

Pitch your tent door away from the wind. Having put up the outer tent (the flysheet), the next best move (as with a bivouac) is to flatten out the insulating pad beneath the groundsheet of the inner tent. It prevents the insulating pad sliding about beneath your sleeping bag when you turn over in the night.

This means you unroll the insulating pad on to the grass first. Then hang up the inner tent, pegging the groundsheet down over and around the insulating pad.

Sort out the rest of your gear in the tent doorway, laying out your sleeping bag inside the tent and stashing anything not needed in camp between the flysheet and inner tent.

If it's raining and the ground is muddy don't worry about dirtying your insulating pad. It keeps you dry whatever the conditions and dries out quickly too.

Your sleeping bag and spare clothing is another matter. If it looks like there's a storm brewing and you sense that a strong wind might even blow everything away, keep these essentials inside your rucksack and plastic bag liner while you set about getting everything else ready – going for water, say – so that once you're lying in your sleeping bag with rain beating down you don't have to go outside again.

Last thing before you get into your sleeping bag to cook the evening's hot meal on a wet night is to check the tent is correctly pitched.

A nylon tent must be pitched so taut that nowhere does the outer tent touch the inner. This way your body vapour condensing on the inside of the flysheet walls cannot come into contact with the inner tent and you keep dry. The tent is also quieter, its fluttering or rattling in the wind cut down to a constant hum instead.

Do remember that cooking in the tent doorway requires care. If you bring the cooker into the tent, boiling water will cover its walls in steam. And if you fry sausages the fat is likely to splatter the tent walls too and damage them. Be sure to hold the pan on top of the cooker with the pan-gripper while your other hand does the stirring or whatever.

Still raining next morning? If you have to move on pack up everything under the flysheet, leaving this till last. You should also swap back to your previous day's clothing, even if still damp, so leaving your spare clothes absolutely dry. This is Outward Bound practice, except in winter. Then it's considered unwise and you just have to take along extra clothing.

To get the best from your tent, if it's packed up wet do unfold it as soon as you return home or reach your next camp site. Damp nylon mildews and rots if left rolled up.

SUPER-BIVVIES

Annual great outdoors events like The Saunders Lakeland Mountain Marathon attract a large following of backpackers and fell runners who compete in the different classes, running over mountains during their hectic weekend and carrying everything they need to camp out the Saturday night on their backs.

Here's now the top men and girls get by with small sacks weighing as little as 10 lb. and less. Their basics are: a tent fly sheet; a heat-reflecting aluminium foil survival blanket (as ground sheet); a down-filled sleeping bag which weighs 3 lb. or less and crushes into the smallest space inside the small-size rucksack; a block of solid camping fuel that heats a solitary pan supported on two rocks; and – for food – muesli mixed with powdered milk and sugar which can be eaten cold or hot. And to drink? Energy-boosting Complan.

SNOW-HOLING

Sleeping inside a snowdrift is fun. The experience is unique and can be part of a camping weekend or holiday. For one night you move higher into the hills, leaving your tent pitched below, much as an Everest climber leaves his base camp. You dig into the snow above the panoramic views below.

A night's snow-holing is considered such a thrill that Glenmore Lodge, the Scottish Sports Council national training centre near Aviemore, includes it as the high point in winter hill-walking courses. Carried out at heights nudging the 1,100 m (3,609 ft) contour in the Cairngorms, it is taught from the point of view of using snow-holes as mobile camping bases rather than a means of survival. At this height, however, the practice is fairly limited to Scotland (and to the Cairngorms in particular).

You need a broad shovel which can be carried strapped to the back of your rucksack and a large-toothed wood saw (or special snow saw). Although you can make an igloo with these tools, the stock snow shelter of good climbers is the snow hole. It is simple and amazingly effective.

Needless to say you also need the full back-up kit of dry clothing, sleeping bag, insulating pad, stove, cooking utensils, food, torch, candles, whistle, map, compass and survival bag, most of which will form part of your usual hill walking apparel and equipment.

You also need a brush for sweeping off bits of snow from your clothing before entering your shelter (a clothes brush is fine). A piece of canvas is needed for placing under your insulating pad, otherwise you will find it shoots out of the snow hole in the night!

Most important for safety, you should always snow-hole in pairs. Choose for your pitch a deep snow-drift that is not exposed to avalanche risk or cornices – that overhanging projection of snow somewhere above formed by the prevailing wind. It pays to remember that snow which is perfect for snow-holing is also good for avalanches, so your snowdrift must be really safe. A useful test is to dig a pit in the snow and examine the separate layers of previous snowfalls. Adjoining layers that differ markedly in hardness are likely to be poorly attached to each other and could slide if disturbed.

Look for a steep drift so that (*a*) it will be deep enough to provide comfortable sleeping space; (*b*) you can, by digging up the slope, simply move all the waste snow downhill with the least effort; and (c) you can quarry snow slabs, then slide them into place like the Egyptians did with the pyramids.

Two people should dig a slot each some 2·10 m high and 1 m wide (7 ft by 3 ft) with about 3 m (10 ft) between the slots. Then join up the two entrances inside the snowdrift and carve out a chamber about 1·80 m (6 ft) high. Cut two sleeping benches, so that you lie in the warmer air (the cold air sinks to the floor). Smooth off the walls with the saw and you should see the different snow layers clearly defined in the walls.

Fill in one entrance with loose snow, banking it down with the shovel. Then roof the remaining slot to within a metre of the floor with snow slabs cut from the adjacent snow slab quarry. The slabs should be about 1·20 m long by 50 cm deep by 30 cm thick (4 ft by 20 ins. by 12 ins.).

Use the saw to cut the slabs, then prise each one out from beneath with the shovel. Simply slide them into place across the slope; the slabs will slide from the quarry quicker if you taper the slab as you go further into the snow.

By leaving the door open you will provide ventilation and give some leeway should there be heavy drifting in the night. (Warning! If you wake in the night to find the candles out and the snow hole really stuffy, get to the door fast with your shovel and start clearing.)

Cut niches in the walls for your candles and place the stove on top of the shovel on the floor with the handle stuck in the wall.

Never cook in a shelter with the door blocked as it could cause a fatal build-up of carbon monoxide. A yellow flame from your candle instead of a blue one is the danger signal.

Also avoid food which needs a long boiling or cooking time, as the steam condenses and makes the walls drip and this could induce a 'great thaw'. For the same reason you must avoid contact with the walls at all costs.

Put your boots in a polythene bag so they won't freeze stiff in the night and keep your digging implements by your side – just in case.

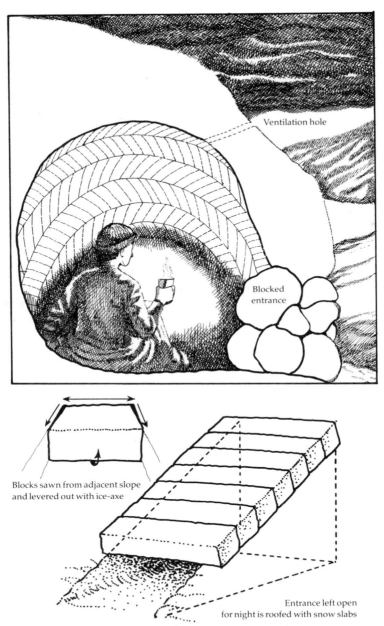

Ventilation hole

Blocked entrance

Blocks sawn from adjacent slope and levered out with ice-axe

Entrance left open for night is roofed with snow slabs

*Two-entrance snow-hole with one entrance blocked, the other semi-roofed with quarried snow slabs*
(Snow layers are, in fact *horizontal* bands formed by successive snowfalls)

Take all your gear into the shelter with you and brush off any loose snow from your clothing before entering the snow-hole, otherwise it will melt with the same consequences as having steam indoors.

Dry clothes are vital inside; it is a good idea to strip off most of your clothing when digging, as even perspiration can make you too damp.

From the outside, the candlelight shows through the snow like fairy lights, but if you wander out to take a peek be sure you can find the entrance again!

# 7

## *Fell Running and Orienteering*

By the year 1997 it is forecast that millions of us will run, cycle or roller skate to school and work. *The Book of Predictions* by David Wallechinsky, Amy Wallace and Irving Wallace goes on to foresee that in 2005 a woman will run a marathon in just over two hours, and that by 2030 the mile will be run in three minutes. Running, in fact, will have gone from strength to strength following the marathon boom.

Running up and down mountains is another sport – a further prophecy ventures – that will greatly increase in popularity through the twenty-first century. Called *fell running* in Britain, *hill racing* in Europe and *mountain marathon running* in America, the sport draws crowds of spectators, who gather in the valley bottoms. However, once the valley has been left behind, the only people you see on the hill are walkers and climbers, and the marshals and mountain-rescue team back-up for the race being run.

Fell running is not alone in being different. Its kindred sport is *orienteering*, navigating around a series of control points scattered over a wide area of open countryside. In orienteering it is not necessary to run, but it helps if you want to win. Otherwise you can still be well-placed at the finish after jogging or even walking around the course.

People who enjoy running frequently discover either fell running or orienteering – and sometimes both – are made for them.

# FELL RUNNING

Eric Beard was a very good climber, killed in a car accident in 1969, but his influence on mountain running remains to this day. He set up many records. He believed fell running was ideal for young people who are competitively inclined and respond to the call of the wild. It is a view that's been proved right as young runners make a point of smashing records.

A twelve-year-old runner from the village where I live in the Lake District runs the half-mile to the top of a 1,500-ft hill in an average time of 14 min. 20 secs. This includes walking some of the way up. But his final time after running back down to the bottom (300 ft above sea-level) is 17 mins. 47 secs. To have a hope of maintaining an average hillside pace like this you must run on hills as much as possible.

It is safer to run with friends. Their presence shadowing your footsteps, or you theirs, makes it more realistic. It helps provide the spur of competition which brings out your best when otherwise you might be too quick to give in, or too timid.

If you live in the north of England or much of Wales or Scotland there will be a good choice of hills for training runs, but in areas like the south of England you must go out of your way to look for them.

As a rock climber will search a mountain just for its crags, and a white water kayak paddler comb a river for its best rapids, you need to scour your local region for usable slopes. It does not matter if they are not very high. So long as they are steep enough to resemble a flight of steps on steep ground you can run up and down them.

Doing things gradually in your running gear is the only way to be safe. This applies even more so if you have the chance of holidaying among mountains when a fell running event takes place that you would like to enter. You will only have a few hours to train. Restrict this to walking up the steep parts of hillsides and down any awkward descents, and jog the rest of the way. Choose a route you think you are capable of doing without too much trouble, and work your training runs up to tougher propositions from that. The best routes are horseshoe-shaped. A skyline is extra good because it swings sharply around so that you are brought back almost to the starting-point as you make your final run downhill, and it will have carried you along its backbone all the way.

EQUIPMENT

To be safe you need a few carefully chosen reserves in case the weather deteriorates or emergencies crop up. What is suitable for hill walking is not always right for fell running – for instance, chocolate which quickly melts in warm weather. Salted peanuts are another example. They prove indigestible when you hurry and provide no quick energy, the quality you need in food that has to be carried. Your best bet here are foods high in glucose, sugar and carbohydrates like the 'energy' bars you can buy in different flavours.

You should carry a pair of thermal long john underpants and your cagoule in a lightweight carrier.

You can use a day sack, preferably with a belt attached to it around your waist to keep it on your back for stability. Most fell runners, however, prefer to wear a specialized 'bum bag'. This is a wide nylon belt, zipped along the top edge of its widest section, which fits snugly against the small of your back and is extremely lightweight.

Bum bag apart, your vest, shorts, ankle socks and fell running shoes are all you require in anything but chilly weather.

Wet and misty conditions are more problematical. You must be careful. Rather than head high for training runs in low cloud, choose instead a lower-level route on safer slopes around the valley bottom. As for competing in these conditions, your only concern is what clothing to wear. If your entry money is accepted for one of the short one-hill events, then to protect yourself against the elements for the relatively short time you will be running, you need shorts worn over your thermal long johns, a long-sleeved thermal vest and your cagoule. A hat and gloves will also help.

Buy a pair of proper fell running shoes as soon as you can afford the considerable amount of money they cost. This can be twice as much as the kind of training shoe you wear at home or school, but they are well worth the extra money.

It is possible to compete in ordinary trainers in fell races. I know because I have done this myself. But the risk of going over on an ankle and suffering twisted ligaments is very real as is the probability of slipping when running downhill and hurting your back. Ordinary trainers also give poor traction when you are trying to thrust your way uphill, and the feel of a foot slipping back on each step is the last thing you want.

A pair of fell running shoes, by contrast, gives the kind of grip racing car drivers expect from their tyres, and not only in dry weather or on springy turf. Fell running shoes will clutch the surface of a muddy slope, a bank of shale, an incline booby-trapped with wet tree roots or rock slabs skiddy with damp lichen.

Most training shoes have unsuitable soles because they are made from materials intrinsically slippery on certain kinds of rough ground. Even fell running shoes, while right for one sort of terrain, can be the reverse for another.

The kind of studs worn under hockey boots are good on the fell in very wet conditions, but not in dry or frosty ones. Metal spikes are used by fell runners on steep grassy courses where there is no road, but the best all-round shoe is the waffle, which has proved successful in several patterns.

The two most popular ones are either a combination of small rubber studs and bars, or alternatively a mat of short stiff plastic bristles that completely cover the underside of the running shoe. The first kind have even been worn on rock climbs.

WHERE TO RUN

There is no kind of terrain which the fell runner discounts if he thinks he can win an advantage by using it. In one of the most famous races, the Guides Race at Grasmere Sports in the Lake District, shepherd Stanley Edmondson once gained on the leader (and favourite), Bill Teasdale, by taking the unusual step of climbing a small crag just below the summit. Teasdale never quite recovered from seeing Edmondson with him at the top when he thought he'd left him behind, and Edmondson beat him in one of the most thrilling finishes ever seen on a mountain race.

It is the downhill dash most of all that distinguishes the fell runner from the cross-country athlete. The steepest sections of mountainside are frequently walked on the ascent simply because it is quicker to walk than to run after a certain angle. It is the only time fell runners do walk.

Running downhill puts great strain on the legs, but the fell runner accepts this and trains for it. He also knows that the eyes fill with tears when conditions are cold or windy, especially just after leaving a summit and just when you need every scrap of good vision for charting the way downhill. This is just one of the many extra problems a downhill dash brings, when continual quick-thinking is more important for your survival than in any other running event.

In Europe many hill races finish on the summit, which is a world away from United Kingdom fell races where running downhill at speed plays a key part in the result.

If you don't feel at home running down steep hillsides, it would be foolish to push yourself into trying too fast too quickly. As the zigzags of your climb up are straightened out by downhill runners bounding straight across their curves, you can imagine the boldness and skill required. The answer is to work at it. Any local slopes you can find are invaluable in this respect. Go up and down them repeatedly to gain that sense of balance and timing which will help you keep your feet on such unnatural ground. It takes nerve, and to gain this takes practice.

*Fell running*

Suppose you have written to the Fell Runners' Association and obtained the fell running calendar (the secretary's name and address can be had from the numerous running and climbing shops in mountain areas). Now you are ready on the start-line of your first fell race, heart steady after a few preliminary jogs up and down a slope to loosen up and warm the blood.

Check the bows of your shoelaces are tied double. This shortens the laces and secures them during the stresses and strains of the run. Many laces come undone and go unnoticed until too late. If you step into a bog and your foot comes out while your shoe stays below the surface you will lose many places just trying to get your muddy footwear back on!

Before you begin running among the mass of elbows, feet and bodies stampeding across the field or up the lane below the hillside waiting beyond, make an agreement with yourself not to try to go too fast at first. *You do not have to keep up with the rest at the beginning of the race.*

Soon enough the field will string out. It is here that those who started off too quickly start to flag while those who got into their stride gradually begin to lengthen it and overhaul those front-runners who did not understand the toll that a mountainside exacts from people too much in a hurry. It is also safer to pace yourself this way. You keep something back in reserve.

## ORIENTEERING

If you like cross-country running, the chances are you will also take to orienteering. This also applies if you jog or ramble. All three have much in common with orienteering.

The going on an orienteering course is similar to the terrain of a cross-country athletic event. The difference is that you can take short-cuts virtually whenever you want.

There is no set course as such. It is up to competitors to

choose their own personal route from one control point to the next. However, it is often the case that the shortest way between two points – that is, from one control marker to the next – is seldom a straight line when orienteering.

Beginners will find that the most certain way of locating their next control point is by taking an easy but possibly roundabout route – say, along a forest road that swings around an area of dense woodland. And when the control is within reach according to your map, you 'attack' it from some feature on the map that gives you your bearings (like a sharp bend in the road). This is why orienteering is such a fascinating activity.

The orienteer who decides to follow his or her compass through the trees along what seems the shortest possible route frequently comes unstuck. If he doesn't lose the way, he loses the control point itself. Turn up at the finish minus a control point where you should have punched your card and extra time is added to the time you took to go round.

The person with the swiftest time wins the event. However, those people who manage to complete the course within a certain period of the winner's time can win badges. To find this required time, just ask the official who accepts your entry money when you register. Knowing there is a badge standard helps spur some people to greater heights.

Rather than the hotshot runner or the competitor with a computer-capability for calculating compass bearings, it is the good map reader who wins hands down in orienteering events. This means simply that, after setting the map as we saw in the chapter on cross-country walking, you work out your best route from the landscape within view, taking into account the features of the map, including the contour patterns.

A good map reader will navigate around an orienteering course hardly ever consulting the compass. All he needs to know is displayed on the map. Here is how to put it to good use.

YOUR FIRST ORIENTEERING EVENT

You might have chosen the event from a list supplied by the British Orienteering Federation (BOF). A useful alternative source is your nearest Sports Council regional office which will be able to give the name of local orienteering club secretaries.

Your event is likely to be held on a Sunday. Many orienteers also take part in other athletic or great outdoor activities on Saturdays. In order that they can have a part of Sunday free, the orienteering event might run from 10.30 am to 2 pm and during this period you can start at any time that suits you.

You also select the particular course most suitable for your experience. Ask the official who takes your entry fee which he recommends. There are two kinds of system in use for identifying these separate courses. Colour-coded courses are popular. The darkest colours are the hardest with brown at the top. White is the easiest of the courses. You might be able to complete this and then have a shot at yellow during the same event for the one fee.

The other method of grading courses is by age. The BOF groups, starting from the bottom (and easiest courses), are: M/W 10 (age 10 and under); M/W 11 (ages 11–12); M/W 13 (13–14); M/W 15 (15–16); M/W 17 (17–18); and so on up to the age of 56 and over.

Orienteers start at one-minute intervals. This is great from the novice's point of view. You feel neither that you have to keep up with anybody else nor that others are breathing down your neck. This staggering of start-times also means that it is very hard to cheat by tagging on behind someone who is running from one control point to another and looking for all the world in top form.

Because your start-time is independent from anybody else's, and also because there are different courses over the same territory for entrants of different ability and experience, you never can be sure which person you see crossing your path is doing what course, short of asking them.

The number of different courses also means that guesswork

is costly in the time you can lose. You are likely to start guessing as you grow more tired. Suppose you are searching fruitlessly for a control point that, according to your information, should be on a small knoll. But there are so many small knolls in sight. None of them appears to sport the bright-coloured three-sided marker which you know you will see once you are 'very warm'. On the point of desperation, you spot a glimpse of orange in the distance on what might be a knoll. Convincing yourself that the marker is the one you need, you run across the rough ground feeling much happier, only to find the number printed on it does not exist on the list of control points that concern your course.

You have mistakenly arrived at a control point belonging to one of the other courses and in a different class entirely. I know very well the dismay you will feel. I have made the same mistake more than once.

To help you keep more on beam, let us look more closely at some of the things which help make life easier.

## ORIENTEERING KIT

A track suit and training shoes are the basic clothing. Alternatively track suit bottoms and a long-sleeved vest or sweat shirt are fine.

You need full arm and leg protection because it has been known to happen that an orienteer with an infectious disease has grazed an arm or leg on brambles when running in shorts and T-shirt. The people following then risk being infected if they also scratch themselves on the same prickly creepers. You carry a compass and whistle on a line around your neck.

How you carry your navigational material is very important too. Here are some tricks the experts use.

## REGISTRATION

At the building, tent or vehicle used as Registration you will receive a map, a controls description list and a control card.

The map is drawn for orienteering. The scale will be large

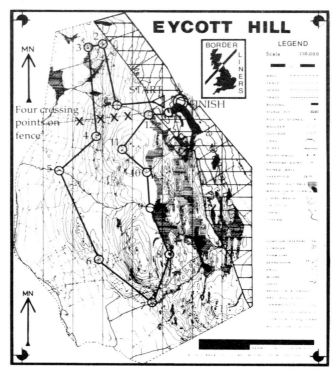

*Orienteering map and accessories*

enough to make it easy for you – say, 1:10,000 (approximately six inches to the mile). Forest may be shown in green and white and open land in yellow and other colours and symbols explained in the map's legend.

The controls description list tells you what the control points of your course will look like and which control point is what number. Landmarks listed are features like stream junctions, boulders, depressions, crags and wall or fence corners.

The control card is a thin strip of card covered with a grid of boxes. Each box bears the number of its control. When you arrive at a control point you carefully press the paper punch you will find there over the appropriate box and prick a pattern of tiny holes to prove you were there.

Fold the map and slide it into your map case with a red

(not Eycott Hill)

| 10 | 1 | CLASS MSOB | | COURSE 11 | | FINISH | | | |
| 11 | 2 | NAME T. GREENOANK | | | | START 12·15 | | | |
| | | CLUB INO. | | | | TIME | | | |
| 12 | 3 | 4 | 5 | 6 | 7 | 8 | 9 | | |
| 13 | 14 | 15 | 16 | 17 | 18 | 19 | 20 | | |

COUNTERFOIL

FINISH — CLASS MSOB START 12·15 — CLUB INO. TIME — NAME T. GREENOANK

Control card and counterfoil
(Appropriate square to be punched at each control point)

Pin punch

Control marker

A

Control Description Card

Red 4.7km.

| Control No | Description | Code |
| --- | --- | --- |
| 1 | Boulder | EN |
| 2 | Boulder N-most | CE |
| 3 | Re-entrant | EL |
| 4 | Gully southern | EK |
| 5 | On the stream | CN |
| 6 | Linear marsh | HO |
| 7 | Southern crag foot | BC |
| 8 | Rocky knoll N-side | CK |
| 9 | Stream | NX |
| 10 | Track bend | BT |
| 11 | Ruin | NV |
| 12 | Outcrop | BE |
| 13 | Knoll | CH |

Follow tapes 100m to finish

pen (red showing up best when you need to draw lines on the map). The controls description list should also be tucked into the map case to keep things together. And the control card? Pin it with two small safety pins to your front so that when you arrive at a control point marker you can – once you have checked its number does in fact belong to the course you are attempting – slip it between the jaws of the punch without unpinning it. Another way to carry the control card is inside the map case, but pinning it to your shirt or vest is quicker.

Another time-saver is to jot down in each of the boxes on your control card a shorthand note of what feature of the landscape you can expect at each control point. This saves you having to consult your controls description list each time you approach a fresh control. A glance at the card pinned on your

front will tell you. For example, in the box for control point
no. 1 you may have jotted 'Bldr'. Immediately you know that
you should be looking for a certain boulder.

After registering for your course, there is one more thing
to do before you go to the start.

### MAP CORRECTIONS

Orienteers make last-minute alterations to their maps in the
Map Corrections area. These are usually zones which a farmer
has requested be placed out of bounds during the event. Or
perhaps you will find details of where a long fence can only
be crossed by specific stiles; these you note on your map to
bring it completely up to date.

### THE PRE-START

Three minutes before the start-time on your control card you
will be checked in on the pre-start line. The official here will
detach the stub on the end of your control card so that Registration then has a record of your attempt. Each minute following this you will move forward one space across a series
of squares until you are on the start-line itself. A whistle
blast tells you each time you should move forward, the final
signal being the one which sets you off from the start-line.

### MASTER MAPS

When the whistle blows that last time you jog along a taped
corridor a short distance towards master copies of each
course. Carefully check which one is yours, then copy down
the course it shows on to your map with your red pen. This
must be done exactly as the master map shows it, including
numbering the small circles you draw precisely around each
control point. You will also need to show the finish exactly as
shown on the master map. Draw the straight lines linking
each control point along the edge of your map case, so that
you can see the correct order of controls at a glance.

## SETTING THE MAP

Before moving off from the master maps and round your course, pause to set the map with the surroundings as we have done previously in this book. Then study the best route you think you should take to the first control.

## DIRECT OR SAFE ROUTES?

Orienteering maps are zoned into Fight, Walk or Run areas depending on the thickness of the forest foliage at those points. That is just one set of choices you have to make. There are others. Do you, for instance, go straight over a hill or round it? As a beginner it will usually pay you to take the longer but safer route at first.

British forests are networked with paths, tracks and rides (or 'fire lanes' where broad avenues between allotments of densely planted trees diminish the risk if they catch fire). Beginners should use these thoroughfares through the trees wherever possible. They can lead you a long way towards your next control if not actually right up to it.

## ATTACK POINTS

An attack point is a definite feature on the map somewhere near a control. The attack point – be it a path junction, boulder, fence corner, crag or bend in the track – gives you something tangible and obvious to go for. You cover the ground quickly to the attack point because it stands out a mile. When you reach the attack point you study the map closely and plan how you will home in on to your control over the next few metres.

## HANDRAILS

The easiest way to cut corners is when you spot on the map a positive 'line' feature of landscape that takes you in the general direction you wish to travel. This can be a stream, wall or earth bank or the fence along the edge of a forest.

Once you have decided where to leave your handrail and strike out on your own for the next control, you can refer to it now and then by keeping it in view rather than following the map in your hand inch by inch.

AIMING-OFF

The same technique you might use on a hill in mist can often be used when orienteering: *deliberately aiming to one side of a control rather than straight at it,* when a line feature such as a fence will then guide you to the actual control lying on it.

If you perhaps wonder how such a technique works on a hill walk think of a bridge over a flooded river in thick mist. Rather than take a compass bearing directly on the bridge, take it a degree or two out to one side. When you reach the river you simply turn right or left, sure in the knowledge that the bridge is not far away along the river bank.

PACING

Orienteers practise counting their double paces (count for one foot only) over a distance of 100 metres and over the different types of terrain you can expect on an orienteering course. This means they can then pace out distances along any compass bearings they take when visibility is poor or landmarks non-existent (as over bleak moorland). Knowing the distance travelled is an enormous help. Although this method is not necessary at first, it does you no harm to try it out whenever you remember.

MAP MEMORY

The less time you spend looking at the map the faster your overall time will be. Make a point of memorizing the map as much as possible. Think: 'Along the track to the third junction, turn right, after a short distance follow the gully to the ruin.' Then put the map away.

It helps to memorize in stages. At first you remember one

fact, then two, then three and so on. What you must not do, however, is try to remember too much at the start. The mind just cannot take it all in and you find your performance suffers accordingly.

The further you progress around a course, the more tired you become, and your thinking is no longer as sharp as it was when you began. Orienteering is said to be the most intellectual of all great outdoors activities. Be ready for this fatigue on the brain. It is very natural. All orienteers know the feeling.

If you find you are running hither and thither like a headless chicken searching for a control that is proving so elusive you feel like giving up, *stop*. Take a bite of any refreshment you may be carrying, then try to piece your map reading together again. The rest can work wonders.

If, however, you become so despondent you decide to throw in the towel halfway around the course you must do one thing. Always report to the Finish to *surrender your control card* and so let the officials know you are safe. This also means you will be more than welcome to try again at another event where your experience of failure might well prove invaluable. Many top orienteers suffer such ignominious starts, only to go on to do great things in the sport which has been described as trying to solve a crossword puzzle while running over hills and through forests.

# 8

## *Lake and River Rafting*

How many of us have longed for a boat, standing by the tempting sight of a glittering lake! Similar thoughts can be stirred by the heavy rainfall which raises the level of a local stream, when you realize it would be possible to voyage down it if only you had a kayak or canoe.

Rafting, one of the oldest forms of travel, makes this possible with the least amount of trouble. You do not need a boat of any kind. All you do is take whatever suitable materials are available, the simplest form of rafting being to lie on top of an airbed and paddle it with your hands!

Whether you raft flat water or float down rapids, you should be able to swim at least fifty metres lightly clothed. You also require a lifejacket or buoyancy aid, warm clothing and – on fast water – a crash helmet. Swiftly-flowing currents down rivers demand head protection. Should you overturn in white water, currents and turbulence could smack you up against a rock with quite a bit of force. If it's your unprotected head that makes contact first, the result could be a bloody fracture.

You also need friends supporting you from the river bank and waiting in positions well down stream just in case . . . They should be equipped with a strong line they can throw to you in any emergency.

# FLAT WATER RAFTING

Outward Bound students learn the main lesson with still water rafting the hard way. Given oil drums, planks and line, they are grouped into teams. First team to make a raft and paddle it across the lake and back wins.

The teams that come unstuck are always those who were in the most hurry to lash everything together and set sail. It is the groups who stop, think and then construct their raft who stand the best chance, though they may not always have the same potential muscle power for the oars.

But what use is your raft when it has fallen apart under the combined weight of all the crew? The thing to remember is that you should not expect too much from a raft. It may need a great deal of adjustment before it sits high on the water. A raft floating on two ten-gallon oil drums, for example, will only just support a grown man as well as its own weight.

A makeshift raft can be constructed from wood, so long as it is dead wood and not living wood you cut down for the purpose. Trees like spruce are best. And build your raft from poles rather than logs, a layer of substantial poles making up the base of the raft and, placed cross-ways on top, a layer of thinner poles giving a platform to sit on.

It's a good idea to test the floating quality of each log separately in water first.

Pointed rafts are easier to propel than square ones. Failing this, a rectangular raft is your best bet, stoutly lashed together with strong cord.

Lashing is crucial when it comes to positioning the buoyancy floats. They need to be tied tightly in place. The advantage of oil drums, large plastic bottles or anything else that floats high in the water is lost when they are left free to wobble about or are not positioned properly.

Buoyancy works best when it is positioned around the edges rather than in the centre of the raft. You also need to add a lot more buoyancy than you need to carry the intended weight of crew.

Oil drums, for instance, must be lashed into position

longways on the raft rather than crossways to the direction of travel. They can be linked in pairs or threes or even between parallel poles, these units then forming each side, say, of a rectangular raft, and separated by the deck sandwiched in between.

Such a craft can be poled along on shallow water or paddled with an oar – or oars – on deep. It can even be sailed with a square sail, though only downwind.

## RAFTING RIVER RAPIDS

The slender, resilient and buoyant platform of a hard-inflated airbed will prove the best support down river rapids. You lie on top, chin down on the pillow, and paddle with your hands along both sides, propelling it downstream through the bends, pools and falls between the river banks.

It will prove more robust than a raft made from oil drums and wooden spars which can break apart along the way. If you hit sharp rocks and come apart, you are left to your own devices in frothing white water.

It is also an improvement on inflatable rubber boats and large rubber tyre inner tubes. These can puncture more easily. The inflatable dinghies bought in surplus stores or from mail order catalogues as surplus military survival rafts are often cheap copies made in Japan or Taiwan and of dubious quality.

There are two other snags inherent in rubber boats and large inner tubes despite the relatively large area of rubber underneath which will make for a reasonably stable craft. Although they will, because of their flexibility, bend and twist over small falls and give on impact with rocks as well as riding over large standing waves, beware! On slower water their ability to flex around mid-stream boulders is a disadvantage. The boat or tyre tends to bend around the rock and hang there. In quiet water such rafts are difficult to manoeuvre because of the surface area they offer the water.

There are raft races all over the world that feature rafts

made of anything from oil drums and wooden spars to large rubber boats, on rivers as varying as the Roaring Fork of the Colorado River, the Colorado River itself where it pours through an eighty-mile section of the Grand Canyon (with twenty sets of big rapids), and the rivers Tay and Tweed in Scotland – not to mention a number of other rivers throughout the United Kingdom.

But in so many cases, and particularly in Britain, the airbed reigns supreme, remaining buoyant and able to cannon off obstacles in its path as it floats on to its journey's end.

Indeed an airbed's passage down a rapid river can be so quick that they have easily beaten support vehicles setting off at the same time and travelling along nearby roads to give assistance if needed further down-river. It has sometimes happened that airbed paddlers have got into difficulties but floated past the point of no return at speed, having to be rescued further downstream.

The more mountainous the region, the better the rafting prospects on airbeds. The annual Glen Nevis Airbed Race directly below Ben Nevis is a good example. The start of the race is a leap with your airbed into a waterfall, then on down into a big pool. It really is great sport!

## HOW TO READ THE RAPIDS

Scout both river banks and inspect the stretch of water you intend rafting on the day you intend travelling. This is your best safety measure. If you content yourself by walking the river bank the evening before, you cannot be sure that fallen trees may not be brought down-current overnight. If you round a bend and face a large tree jammed across the main channel you are in trouble because you could be swept underneath and have to fight to escape the mantrap of branches.

Watch out too for banks thick with willow trees, and weirs. You will need to give them a wide berth on your way down the water.

It's safer and more fun if several of you raft a river together. Let someone know where the group is going. Better still, have people on the banks in the role of support and rescue group.

Solo rapid river rafting is asking for trouble. Rapids ahead can be spotted by their noise, a silvery line across the waterway and quiet water immediately above them. A canoeist unsure of what lies ahead would land and examine the river from the bank. So should the rafter.

Below some rapids there are stopper waves. These are so called because of their effect on rafts and canoes when water flows over a large rock and then, with the increased pressure, flows back on itself, breaking like a wave at sea and stopping the forward movement of any craft unlucky enough to hit it at the wrong point.

However, on a river the stopper wave does not move. It just stays there like a haystack of white water forever menacing the unwary paddler. To swim in a stopper is dangerous and like being tumbled around in a washing machine. Often the only way is to dive and swim out from beneath it.

So instead of simply freewheeling in rapid water, try to go faster than the current by paddling with both hands. This gives some semblance of control. You can avoid obstacles ahead by paddling extra hard on one side of the airbed so that you veer away from the danger immediately facing you.

When water flows away from you in a glassy-looking 'V' funnel, aim right down the middle. It means you will then slip easily between the rocks setting up that natural channel in the first place.

Avoid where possible large powerful eddies circling alongside a strong current. You may not have the horsepower to pull clear. A good way to experiment with this is to carry a plastic bucket and line on board. Just toss the bucket into the main current and hang on as it drags you from the eddy at speed.

One of the top kayak paddlers in Britain says: 'Only experience can teach you how to judge a rapid. In general, though, the main flow of the current will be through the deepest channel. Your canoe or raft will then be carried through the best route quite naturally. This is why checking these channels from the riverbanks is so important for your safety at first. If a channel obviously heads into danger, then you should stop well in advance of that particular piece of rough water and carry your craft around it.'

However successful your trip down rapids may prove, it will be spoiled if you encounter angry fishermen along the way. Fishing rivers in the UK are seriously restricted to all canoeists. The same applies to rafters. It is always best to check locally if there is likely to be any objection to your paddling a particular river or stream. A 'rogue' trip may spoil it for canoeists who, through their clubs or the British Canoe

*Using fast water for fun*
(arrows show direction of current)

**A.** Lying on an airbed in an eddy, try throwing a plastic bucket into the current.
Result: when the bucket is whipped downstream you are dragged out of
the slack water (dotted figure) INTO SAFE POOL DOWNSTREAM   **B.** Shooting a rapid on an airbed

*Airbed rafting with helmet, buoyancy aid, and wet suit and boots*

Union, agree that they will only paddle the water at certain times of year. Respecting such rulings and looking elsewhere for a piece of quick current to ride is a sensible course of action.

# 9

## Flat and White Water Canoeing

Fill a canoe almost full with buckets of water and you can carry out a most interesting experiment. The canoe must be a kayak with single cockpit containing the in-built kind of buoyancy that makes it unsinkable even when full of water. Climb inside, take a paddle and propel yourself and canoe into the middle of a pond or river which you know is safe because you have already swum in it.

Paddle the boat forwards so the water inside the canoe swills backwards towards the stern, then, reversing your paddle strokes, paddle the boat backwards to make the water inside change direction and begin to move towards the bows in a forwards motion. Repeat the sequence, travelling forwards then backwards several times until you feel the bows beginning to dig deep into the water because of the thrust of the heavy mass of water moving inside and building up such a momentum it acts like a powerful piston inside the canoe.

Paddling even harder now to increase the nosedive, the rear of the canoe will climb up out of the water and the canoe will stand up vertically before toppling over loop-the-loop style and landing on the surface of the water upside down. You can either Eskimo-roll back to the surface with your paddle if you are an expert or – as a beginner – you bale out from the cockpit, swim to the surface, grab your paddle and tow the canoe by the bows or stern back to the side for emptying out before you have another go.

I make no apology for starting this chapter on the serious outdoor activity of canoeing with this trick. It simply makes a very important point. Many people consider canoeing fun

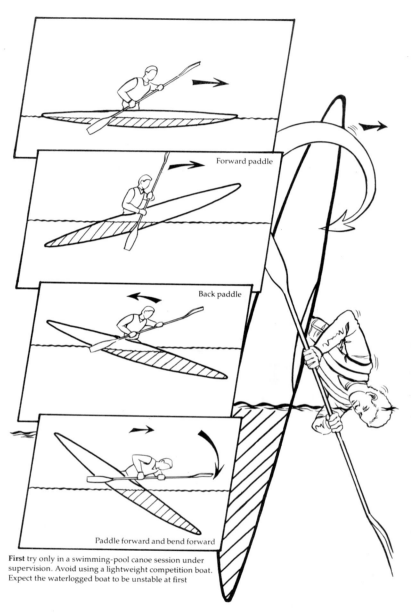

Forward paddle

Back paddle

Paddle forward and bend forward

**First** try only in a swimming-pool canoe session under supervision. Avoid using a lightweight competition boat. Expect the waterlogged boat to be unstable at first

*How to loop the loop in a canoe*

before they have actually paddled a canoe. They can be in for a rude awakening.

People who make good at canoeing like water. They revel in swimming underwater, diving, and tricks like looping a canoe which actually is a legitimate technique performed by experts on river rapids and in ocean surf, though with the canoe quite dry inside.

If you do not like water particularly, if you can swim but still do not like to venture out of your depth, then no matter how much you may yearn to canoe in future, you should first visit your local swimming baths and make yourself at home in water. Once you begin to enjoy your swimming so much that you look forward to it you can think about canoeing.

Once more I must repeat that canoeing is a serious activity. The paddler in the cockpit, whether on flat water or rapids, is in effect soloing – something no inexperienced rock climber would dream of doing. There is no rope to save you if you capsize and your head fails to surface quickly. You must be able to swim fifty metres lightly clothed and feel confident and cool-headed if your head has to stay underwater for several seconds.

The modern sporting canoe will allow you to get the most out of paddling rapids and surf, but it does have a small cockpit and a restricted feeling around the legs once you have slid them inside. The feeling can be claustrophobic if you are constantly worrying about how you will get out if you capsize.

In a moment we will see how getting out of the canoe after a capsize is the first thing to learn. It is a most important part of canoeing and you cannot practise it sufficiently at first.


## CANOES AND CANOEING EQUIPMENT

I am not going to suggest any special canoe or specific equipment. It is more necessary at first to gain experience so that when the time comes to invest in a costly item like a canoe it is exactly right for the kind of canoeing you have in mind. It is easy to make an expensive mistake here and to purchase a canoe which proves unsuitable as your increasing experience outruns it.

The modern kayak is a slim fibreglass or plastic pod weighing well under 30 lb. and with just enough room for your legs to slide under the decks and your bottom to fit the bucket seat. It has been developed from the Eskimo skin boat, which was built from sealskin or walrus hide stretched over a wooden frame and used for hunting and fishing in rugged Arctic seas. Modern plastic and fibreglass methods have enabled the Eskimo design to be converted into a finely tuned and competitive boat. It is propelled by a twin-bladed paddle.

The alternative is the white water or decked canoe. This is a relatively recent development which is a cross between the traditional open canoe and the kayak. White water canoes are decked over apart from the cockpit holes in which the paddlers kneel using a one-bladed paddle.

You can buy a kayak or canoe new or second-hand for half to two-thirds the price. Although fibreglass boats can be made at home from kits, they are usually poorer in quality, heavier in weight and generally not as up to date in design as the professionally-manufactured product. Wood and canvas boats are fragile and heavy and lack the performance of a craft made from modern materials.

There are a number of ancillary items which should complement the boat you eventually buy. You will need a lifejacket or buoyancy aid (the buoyancy aid is the choice of the vast majority of canoeists), paddles, crash helmet (for shooting rapids), spray deck (a watertight canopy which fits round the waist and snaps on to the cockpit rim), a large sponge for mopping up water, and appropriate clothing.

As for any other great outdoors activity, it's advisable to wear several layers of lightweight clothing so they can be shed or added to at will. It's the top half of the body that will be exposed to the elements, so wear a windproof jacket and some kind of hat on flat water in cool weather. For the rest, thermal long johns or shorts and training shoes are best because they won't hamper you if you have to swim for it.

Experienced canoeists wear a sleeveless wet suit during the winter months but it's not a necessary item for beginners.

## HOW TO START CANOEING

You can choose from river, canal and lake touring, rapid river running, competing in slalom competitions on rough water, and wild water racing down stretches of fast river containing rapids. There is also sea canoeing, with surf canoeing having its own special appeal.

I have no doubt at all that to take even a short course will help you immensely to decide on the kind of canoeing you prefer. It is even better if you join your local canoeing club after following your course, thereby building up your experience and expertise in the right hands and in the stimulating company of other canoeists.

There are clubs throughout Britain which are affiliated to the British Canoe Union (BCU). These clubs offer training in the basic techniques. When the student is ready, he can take the BCU star test with certificates and badges which require him to conform to an established standard of safe watermanship.

However, if you have access to a canoe, paddles, a lifejacket or buoyancy aid and shallow, sheltered and safe water, you can take certain tentative first steps at once, bearing in mind that practice does not always make perfect and you might well use techniques and unknowingly pick up bad habits that make canoeing hard work. There is no substitute for qualified instruction. Try your hand out in a canoe in the company of friends by all means but do not forget the value of proper coaching from the beginning.

Secondly, most fishing rivers in Britain are severely restricted for canoeing. The local British Canoe Union River Adviser, whose name is available from BCU headquarters, will advise you which landowners and angling societies to approach for permission if you happen to live near this kind of water. In the case of larger navigable rivers and canoe touring, you should apply to the local river board for a permit. Approach the Inland Waterways Board for canals.

## THE FIRST TIME ON THE WATER

You require flat water – the proverbial millpond. It may be slow flowing and shallow, but make sure it is not polluted. In some parts of the country a capsize can result in more serious injuries than a mere soaking. A river used as a drain by a local chemical factory can cause serious damage to internal organs if you happen to swallow the water. A canoeist who regularly canoed across one river to work found the gelcoat of his boat was disappearing. If polluted water can do that to a canoe then you should be doubly careful about checking for this danger with the local water authority.

By contrast, clay pits and gravel pits often found in reclamation schemes can be very clean. A local pond or quiet stretch of unpolluted river will also be ideal.

### CARRYING THE CANOE

To lift a single-seater, grip the cockpit with both hands under the nearest edge and lift on to one knee. Now change hands to grasp the far side of the cockpit and lift the canoe on to your shoulder, keeping the upper arm inside.

### GETTING IN

Before actually taking your canoe on to the water, you must first master getting inside it! Put your boat on the slowest-flowing water you can find. It should not be tried on fast-flowing water until you have gained experience. Wear a lifejacket or buoyancy aid as it is possible to fall in before you take a single paddle stroke.

Face the boat upstream, then place your paddle across and between the back of the cockpit and the bank. This gives you a stable bridge between the two. By holding the paddle loom (its shaft) with one hand and the back of the cockpit with the other, and keeping your weight over towards the bank, you can slide both legs down into the boat from a really stable position.

It is a good idea to keep the legs straight. Then, before you begin paddling, check that your feet touch the footrests and your knees can press underneath the deck while sitting comfortably in the seat. Five firm points of contact will let you feel you are 'wearing' the boat rather than rattling about inside it without support.

When you are ready to enter even the slowest current, the reason you pointed the canoe upstream becomes obvious. It allows you to hold your own against the flow and to work up slowly into the moving water that you can see. If you faced downstream instead, it would take some moments to gain control of the boat, in which time you might be swept into any one of numerous kinds of obstacle.

CAPSIZING PRACTICE

Capsize drill is often carried out in swimming baths. Outdoors, however, you need a warm day, a change of clothing and towel so you don't hang around feeling chilled afterwards. Try as many capsizes wearing your buoyancy aid as you are capable of. This is the most important part of canoeing, and you should become familiar with it before you paddle a single stroke other than the few movements you make with your arms in the water to push your boat away from the bank.

A friend standing in the water by the canoe is a common-sense safety measure. If you had difficulty freeing yourself from the cockpit, he would be on hand to haul you and the canoe upright at once. Undignified, yes, but safe.

If the boat has a spraydeck to seal the cockpit, do not wear it. You do not require a spraydeck for a little while.

The most important thing to remember when your head goes underwater (with you holding your nose if you wish) is to relax. If you try to raise your head above water the moment after it becomes submerged, your legs will still be inside the boat. You will bale out, but with a struggle, and your legs are likely to be bruised by the cockpit coaming.

A better way is to *enjoy* hanging upside down in the cockpit for a moment then, pressing both hands just behind the hips on the deck, leave the cockpit with an easy forward roll motion, legs straight.

Do not try to right the boat as you return to the surface. It will fill with water and become unmanageable. Simply swim to either end and hold on by the toggle fitted there, then swim to a convenient bank and empty out the water.

It is well worth always carrying out capsize drill in any canoe you come to paddle in the future. You might try a sleek competition boat with a small cockpit with someone who is an experienced canoeist standing by to help. They will almost certainly insist you capsize the boat before doing anything else, no matter how many hours you have previously paddled in a kayak with a more roomy cockpit.

## HOLDING THE PADDLE

Once inside the cockpit, and knowing you can get out of it quickly and safely, you are ready to begin paddling. It helps if you have the right size of paddle from the start.

When the paddle is held upright, you should be able to reach up over the top of it, arm fully raised, and just curl your fingers over the tip of the blade.

Hold on to the paddle loom with arms elbow-width apart. This gives a comfortably powerful surge to your paddling stroke. A lot of novices tend to hold their hands too close together. The idea is to grasp firmly with one hand and allow the loom to slide easily in the other. This is because kayak paddles are set at right angles to allow the blade out of the water to feather edge on to the wind rather than flat face on and so cause wind resistance.

To find which hand you prefer to control or fix the paddle, sit in the cockpit and try twisting the paddle loom as you make imitation paddle strokes.

Right-handed people will use their right hands to control the feathering, the top of the hand always at right angles to the right paddle blade. After drawing this blade through the water, the back of the right hand angles sharply upright and then backwards as it turns the loom so the other paddle blade then enters the water at the correct angle. During this angling of the back of the control hand, the other hand allows the loom to slip round without trying to grasp it in any way.

### THE FORWARD PADDLE STROKE

Pushing the control hand straight out in front of you from the shoulder, you then lower the blade and draw it back through the water. This action enables your other paddle blade to be at full stretch of the other arm, which is then lowered into the water in similar fashion and pulled back, so making possible paddle strokes on both sides of the boat in steady succession.

Avoid trying to pull too much on the loom. It is a two-handed operation, one hand punching forward to the full extent of the arm, the other pulling back. Done correctly it will save you a painfully sore back.

Last of all remember that the paddle is drawn close to the boat. The moment you begin getting the paddle blades further away, you start turning the boat from a straight course.

### BACKWARDS PADDLING

Starting on your control hand side again, sweep the blade back so it enters the water behind hip level and pull it forwards. As you alternate between left and right, glance over your shoulder to the stern of the boat so that you are aware in which direction the boat is moving.

### BRAKING

If you need to stop your boat rather quickly dig the right and left paddle blades into the water, holding them vertically. Backwards paddle by heaving forward on the paddle blades equally hard on both sides of the boat so you don't begin to go broadside on to the current. There is another application to this technique, as we will see in a moment (the ferry glide).

## THE SWEEP STROKE

The basic move used to change direction, to turn your boat right round from a stationary position, or to correct the bows from swinging over-much from side to side as you paddle forwards, is the sweep stroke. The difference between this and the ordinary forward paddling stroke is that the paddle blade is placed in the water further forward, with the loom held lower, so that you are able to sweep the paddle round in a large arc to finish right at the back of the boat. The paddle needs to be held well out over the water so a good arc is possible and as far away from the boat in the middle of the arc as possible.

## THE ESKIMO ROLL

Capsizing a kayak and then righting it without leaving the cockpit might seem for experts only. However, it has an important application other than the survival one of bobbing back upright in rapids, when to swim would be more dangerous than to Eskimo-roll.

Today most competent canoeists who have to tackle rough water have mastered the technique which was used for centuries by Eskimos to right a capsized kayak in open sea. It is a most valuable aid to training.

Once you can Eskimo-roll, you will also be able to use a range of recovery strokes which will support your boat at all angles as you brace yourself on the paddle and lean right out over the current.

The Eskimo roll should be learned under safe and comfortable conditions. A number of BCU clubs give rolling instruction in indoor swimming pools. When you can execute the roll in a swimming bath, you can progress outdoors to still water and eventually fast-flowing rivers.

There are various techniques for rolling in which the

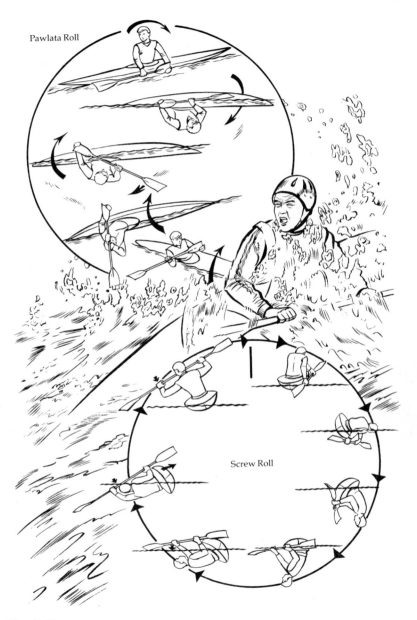

Pawlata Roll

Screw Roll

*Two Eskimo Rolls*

canoeist leans either backwards or forwards and rotates the boat by using the paddles. Good canoeists can roll using just their hands.

Very briefly, the roll is not the magic technique it might appear. But to do it well, it will help if you like water and feel confident in it.

The paddle is moved into a position parallel with the canoe after you have breathed in enough air to see you through. Then, when you are upside down in the water, the paddle is brought into play again on the other side of the boat.

Once the paddle emerges the paddler sweeps it in an arc across the top of the water, with the blade at an angle to the water so that it planes across the surface. At the same time, by a combination of a strong flicking movement with the hips and pressing on the paddle loom, the canoeist can surface once more, streaming with water and regaining control in a matter of moments.

As you would be wearing a spray deck, the inside of the canoe stays dry. If you wear glasses they will stay on if you tie a piece of elastic tape from each ear piece and round the back of the head.

### THE FERRY GLIDE

At this stage of your very basic introduction, if you want to avoid an obstacle ahead you can make the current do the work. This technique is known as the ferry glide.

You simply hold yourself stationary in mid-current by back-paddling on both sides, making sure you do not go broadside on to the current. This is the one position in which your boat is most prone to capsizing, so try to keep it more or less in line with the current.

If there are rocks ahead and you wish to pass well over to the right, then swing your stern at an angle across the current so that it points to the right. Hold the position, keep back-paddling and the current will move you sideways towards the right bank and exactly where you want to be.

## RIVER TOURING

The ferry glide is a technique you will use a lot on your first trips down a river. Rather than voyaging on such an excursion on your own, it is much better to go with a canoeing club. It is safer all round and you will learn so much more, from how to assess rapids before trying to shoot them to which stretches of river are sensitive when it comes to angling clubs and need advance permission to canoe them.

## WILD WATER RACING

Racing down rapids in kayaks and canoes one at a time is one of the possibilities when you become more experienced. There are races on rivers all over Britain, whose organizers have obtained permission to canoe that particular section of water.

## CANOE SLALOM

Slalom canoeing was a competition event in the Olympics. It is *the* test of manoeuvrability, racing your boat between poles the same as a ski slalom. You not only go down and across rivers but upstream as well! You also have to reverse through some gates backwards with continual glances over your shoulder as your boat is pounded by the boiling water. The only way not to penalize yourself if you capsize is to roll up again.

Slalom, the ultimate in boat control in rough water, is one of the great sports. It is very competitive and requires a high degree of technique, fitness and courage.

## SEA SURFING

Rough sea or sea surfing means driving your canoe into the foaming surf and is for experts only. There are competitions here as well. Sea canoeing in its broader sense is becoming more popular, for coastal journeys and channel crossings.

Sea canoeing calls for an understanding of tidal factors and a knowledge of navigation. It is also essentially a group activity. A paddler who failed to roll in cold sea water and had to bale out would be lost without companions to help him right, empty and re-occupy the stricken boat.

Wild water racing . . . slalom canoeing . . . sea surfing . . . they are all in the future, of course. Nor are they the limit of what you can do. There is also long-distance racing and sprint racing on flat water. But there are many techniques to learn first, whichever kind of canoeing you may specialize in as your experience increases. Whatever you choose, canoeing will allow you to see places in Britain and around the world, frequently from the surface of water normally not voyaged by anyone save canoe paddlers.

# 10

## *Rock and Ice Climbing*

Much rock climbing practice is possible on boulders, embankments, bridges, buildings, quarries and climbing walls built for climbers at ground level. The Currie Walls near Edinburgh, Finnieston Dock near Glasgow, Horspath Bridge near Oxford and the boulders of Central Park, New York, are examples. They are typical of what you find in virtually any city or town if you look sufficiently hard.

Practice on these will prepare you for mountain crags and sea cliffs where your rock climbing begins in earnest and for ice climbing on the highest and most striking mountain crags of all.

For climbing ice you use similar movements to climbing rock, but it is of course harder to practise ice climbing at low levels. Good ice usually forms only at high altitudes on mountain crags. These are the same rock faces popular in summer, but in winter they are shrouded in smears of thick ice, frozen waterfalls and refrigerated cascades.

Rock and ice climbing are enjoyable sports. They do not ask a great deal in advance. Both use natural movements of the body and neither requires lengthy instruction. However, they do need more than a modicum of common sense. And this calls for some tuition in the first instance.

## ROCK CLIMBING

A short rock climbing course makes a good start. Rock climbing is a team activity with two climbers sharing one rope and certain pieces of equipment.

What better way than for you and a like-minded friend to take such a course together? Or, better still, for four of you to do this? That would make two teams – two ropes of two climbers who add to their personal safety by visiting crags together. Each pair of climbers can then keep in touch on neighbouring routes at the same time.

Here are the kind of things you can learn on such a course, even before you have bought any equipment.

### BOULDERING

Wearing track suits and training shoes, you may be shown a number of entertaining and instructive rock-climbing problems centimetres from the ground on a variety of surfaces from the walls of buildings and gardens to low rock outcrops. Ropes are not used because you don't try to climb up. Instead you are shown how to step sideways from foothold to handhold and handhold to foothold in the same way you would move around and just above the surface of a deep pool on a mountain gorge walk.

If you feel you are going to fall you simply step back down to the ground. Besides teaching you a lot about placing (and trusting) your feet on all kinds of footholds, this also strengthens your fingers and arms.

### TOP-ROPING

The expression 'top-roping' means that as a beginner you will be taken to a small, friendly crag and there taught rock climbing with the safety of a rope from above. This allows you to make the mistakes all novices make yet be near the ground and in perfect safety. The same technique can be used once you leave the course and find a low practice crag in your home vicinity.

Thousands of Outward Bound students have top-roped Diamond Crag and Rank's Bank in the Lake District. Welsh climbers begin on a group of rocks called The Pinnacles opposite the post office in Capel Curig, and in America the 600-ft cragface of Lover's Leap near Strawberry, a Greyhound bus flagstop along US Highway 50 in the Sierra Nevada mountains of California, has given similar opportunities to young climbers top-roping the satellite outcrops near its base.

The technique used is the same the world over with one or two small variations depending where you are. I am sticking to the simplest of them all, on crags no taller than 30 or 40 ft.

Track suit and trainers are fine, though you may be provided with climbing boots. Certain pieces of personal kit are issued to you, which you alone use on each little climb. They are items you will become familiar with if you go on to take up rock climbing seriously. They are: a climbing belt; two screw-gate karabiners (the metal clip that looks like a chain link which is used by climbers for a variety of reasons and which opens up along one side with a gate that snaps shut with the click of a camera shutter); a stitch plate through which you control the rope; and a climbing helmet.

The system you use will be to climb in pairs, two people to their own route up the rock. You climb up one route and back down it, then protect your partner as he climbs up and down it, then move on to the next climb and so on until you have both completed the half dozen or so routes available for the morning or afternoon session.

Picture yourself standing below the first climb.

Let us say it is a chimney which it resembles save that one side is open to the daylight. Peering up inside you think you can see a way of climbing it.

The instructor will climb first to show you how to do it, after he has first tied one end of the climbing rope to his own climbing belt or harness. As he tows the rope up the climb, it hangs down behind him to the coils lying on the ground where he left it before beginning.

At the top of the climb, he loops a nylon tape sling around a convenient tree and clips the two ends together with a karabiner. Threading the rope through this, he returns by climbing back down the chimney, still towing the rope after him.

The climb is now set up for the rest of the session and the instructor will go on to rig the remaining little climbs with separate ropes in similar fashion. Everyone can now climb these short rock problems with the benefit of a strong rope and pulley protecting their every move from above.

### THE SAFETY PULLEY SYSTEM

At each end of the rope now hanging doubled down your chimney the instructor ties a figure-of-eight knot. It is the simplest knot and the only climbing knot you need to know for now.

Let us call your partner Chris. It's time for both Chris and you to put on your climbing belts. Work the pointed end of your belt through the buckle, and continue feeding it through until the belt feels comfortable and tight around the waist. Then force the end of the belt back through the buckle a second time and draw it really tight to make sure it cannot slip.

Taking one of the screw-gate karabiners, clip this on to your climbing belt after pulling the belt buckle well over to one side of your waist to get it out of the way. Then clip one of the knotted ends of the rope into the karabiner and screw up the lock on the gate.

After Chris has clipped on to the other end, you might toss a coin. You won? Then you climb first.

Shown how by the instructor, Chris pulls the rope through the karabiner above until all the slack has gone and you feel it tug your climbing belt. Chris then clips a second screw-gate (karabiner) on to his own belt and prepares to control the rope through it so that you will be safe. This he does by pushing a small U-bend of rope through the slot in the stitch plate as shown in the diagram. Clipping the little U-bend into the karabiner, Chris feeds the rope through the stitcht plate, round the karabiner and out through the stitcht plate again as you climb.

The result is that the rope keeps pace with you. All the time you feel it tugging lightly at your waist.

By feeding the rope smoothly through the stitcht plate slot with one hand, and round the karabiner with the other, Chris's action is not unlike somebody trying to start a chainsaw or powerboat's outboard motor.

It is this 'pulling through' hand which, if you slipped, Chris would draw back sharply as if trying to give either of those motors an extra flip of the starting cord. And the rope locks in the stitcht plate, preventing you from falling further.

On a real rock climb there is a danger that a rope-handler doing this might be lifted off his feet by the velocity of the other climber's fall. In that case both climbers would be at risk. And to prevent this ever happening the rope-handler would not only be tied, or *belayed*, to the rock face, but belayed in such a way that he could not be lifted off his feet by the pulley effect of a rope running through a karabiner overhead.

Now you've reached the top, here is how to descend.

Holding on to the rope in front with both hands, and with the instructor watching over Chris as the rope is held tight, you lean right back. Chris now feeds the rope out slowly through the stitcht plate, this time paying it out rather than – as when you climbed – taking it in. As he lets out the rope bit by bit, so you descend with feet flat on the rock, leaning out into space backwards.

This sounds sensational. It feels sensational. It *is* sensational! But as long as Chris controls the rope with his 'pulling through' hand, you will be able to step backwards down the outer edge of the chimney in total safety. (And of course the instructor sees that Chris performs this manoeuvre correctly.)

At the bottom you swap roles. Chris unclips the rope from the karabiner and pulls it out from the slot in the stitcht plate. You meanwhile haul in all the slack rope through the karabiner above until the rope pulls on your partner's waist. Then you push a small U-bend of rope through the stitcht plate slot and around the second karabiner with which you were issued. You are ready to safeguard your friend.

When he has been up and down again and when you have unclipped the rope from your belts, you can move on to the next climb, leaving the rope hanging down for the next climbing team.

ABSEILING

Abseiling means sliding down a fixed rope by making use of the principle you have just seen at work: namely, a sharp U-curve in the rope round a karabiner or other object will create enough friction to check a falling body when an extra bend is put in the rope to create an S-bend.

The abseiling session on a course might take all day. This shows how serious it is. You cannot afford to make a mistake when abseiling. Unlike the climbing where you hold on to the *rock*, and the rope is only there in case you fall, in abseiling you hold on to the *rope*. If that fails there is no back-up. You would fall.

During a climbing course or in the company of an experienced instructor you will always wear a safety rope at first. If you made an error and fell, the safety rope would field you.

Left to your own devices on a crag, just you and a friend, if you *had* to abseil – in other words a climb was proving too difficult and you decided to retreat by abseiling – it is unlikely you would have a safety rope. Were you to make a serious mistake and fall, it would be like having a parachute that didn't open.

Abseiling is as serious as that. It looks fun on television, but you must never treat it casually.

The most basic form of abseiling requires no other kit than the rope, a strong anchor and your own body. However as a beginner you will wear a climbing belt and karabiner, and be linked to this by a separate safety rope which the instructor – belayed safely – will pass through a stitch plate as you make your way down the steep rock.

The abseil rope will be doubled around a tree or rock at the

*The basic 'classic' abseil protected by a safety rope handled by another climber*

top of the crag and hang down in two halves in much the same way as it did during your top-roping practice sessions. Rather than starting from the bottom, however, you begin abseiling at the top.

Once attached to the safety rope, you stand astride the doubled rope with your back to the view down the rock. With both hands lift the doubled rope as high as possible up between the legs, then – if you are right-handed – bring both ropes together around the back of the right thigh. Carry on feeding the rope diagonally up across the front of your body so it then passes squarely over your left shoulder, diagonally down behind your back and into your right hand.

Double-check the position. Your left hand holds the rope in front of you as a balance-aid at the start. To stop, you simply move the rope in your right hand across the front of your stomach.

Stopping is not the problem, as you will discover. It's starting off that is difficult. The friction of the S-bend of rope round your body is so great you have to force yourself against its resistance.

The classic abseil is something you would only fall back on in a crisis, but it should still be among the first kinds of abseil you are taught if you intend making a go of climbing. The other abseils involve wearing some form of sit-harness and a figure-of-eight descendeur device through which the rope makes an S-bend rather than going round your body.

There are also abseils where the rope passes through various systems of karabiners. You will learn to do the basic ones during your climbing course.

Before you reach this stage, perhaps you should bear in mind the kind of things that can happen when abseiling if you allow your concentration to wander.

The following incidents happened to climbers who didn't think. The rope was not long enough to reach a ledge below and the climber abseiled off the end and into space; a sharp edge chopped the abseil rope, when the climber's weight came on to it abruptly; a climber's long hair was trapped between the rope and the metal descendeur and he could

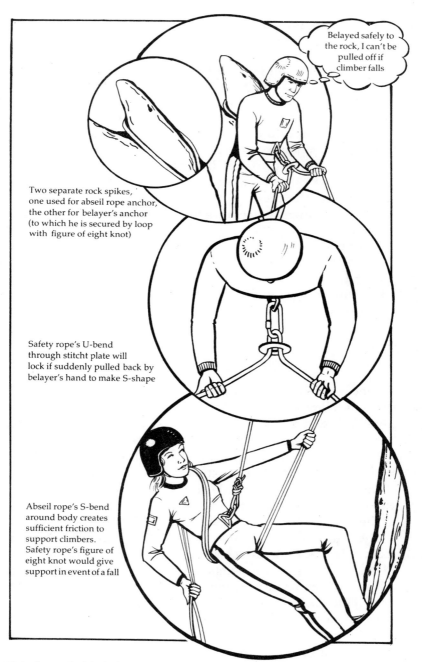

Two separate rock spikes, one used for abseil rope anchor, the other for belayer's anchor (to which he is secured by loop with figure of eight knot)

Safety rope's U-bend through stitcht plate will lock if suddenly pulled back by belayer's hand to make S-shape

Abseil rope's S-bend around body creates sufficient friction to support climbers. Safety rope's figure of eight knot would give support in event of a fall

*This shows the kind of rock anchors used for belays; the basic climbing knot (the figure of eight); and how an S-bend of rope creates a friction that works*

move neither up nor down; the rope slipped off the spike of rock which was supposed to be the anchor; climbers faced with a series of abseils to retreat from a climb during an electric storm both reached the safety of a ledge halfway down, then found their rope had stuck and could not be pulled down after them by tugging one end as is the usual technique; a climber rested on a tiny ledge in mid-abseil, but when his weight came off the rope, the release of tension sent a ripple running up the rope which then rode up and slipped off its anchoring rock spike . . . And these are only some of the things which have happened when an abseil goes wrong.

I always take it easy when abseiling, and double-check every move, though by now I know them off by heart. I cannot help feeling conscious that many celebrated climbers have come to grief on this one particular technique where so much depends on factors outside the climber's immediate control.

MULTI-PITCH ROCK CLIMBS

The next step in your climbing initiation is to tackle several separate climbing problems similar to those posed by the little rock climbs you completed first of all on a top-rope. Now, however, the short climbs are stacked up high one on top of another to make up one long rock climb. And you climb them by the same sequence climbers use the world over.

By ascending the first little climb and landing on the ledge above it, you are ready for the next, and the next. And so on to the top, via perhaps as many as half a dozen such stages.

The 'little climbs' are called *pitches*; the ledges in between, *stances*. These you treat as solid ground. They are the meeting places where the two members of a climbing team pair up and belay before proceeding with the next pitch. Belay? If you remember, I mentioned this earlier. It means tying yourself to the cragface so you cannot be pulled off should your partner take a fall.

The most common form of belaying where you are rock

climbing, scrambling, caving or gorge walking roped together is the simple figure-of-eight knot. You tie this in the rope at about arm's length and carefully loop it over and around a suitably sound spike or flake of rock. I give 'at around arm's length' as a rule of thumb. The key thing is that your belay is taut. A taut belay will hold you firmly when you need it. A slack belay will allow you to be whipped off your feet, possibly losing control of the rope in the process.

The sequence of a rock climb begins with the leader spearheading the way up the first pitch, just as your instructor led the way up that initial chimney during top-rope practice.

There is just one difference. From the start, on a rock climb the second climber (the *second*) pays out the leader's end of the rope through a stitcht plate. This is in case the leader places *running belays* or *runners* on the pitch he is climbing. I will go into running belays in a moment, but for now you can take it that your stitcht plate will be in constant use during the climb.

On reaching the first stance the leader belays himself and calls: 'On belay!' This lets you know he is safe and that you can free the rope from the stitcht plate and karabiner, the leader meanwhile calling: 'Taking in!' and pulling in the slack.

In return you shout: 'That's me!' as the rope finally pulls on the climbing belt.

After a long pause as the leader positions the rope through the stitcht plate slot and into a karabiner, he calls: 'Climb when you're ready . . .' to which, setting hand and foot on the rock, you reply loudly: 'Climbing!'

Overhead the leader reassures with an 'Aye, aye' or 'OK', and you start up. If you don't also feel the physical reassurance of the rope being taken in as you climb, but instead the rope hangs slackly down in an ever-growing loop as you climb, call 'Take in!'

What often happens instead is the rope pulls too tightly. In which case you call 'Slack!'

On reaching his stance, the leader will belay you to a suitable rock anchor. This need not always be a spike.

Sometimes it's a rock that has jammed in a vertical crack and which is mechanically sound. In that case he loops a sling or the climbing rope around this 'chockstone'; you will learn techniques as you progress.

After waiting while you slot the leader's rope through your stitcht plate, the leader removes his own belay and begins to climb the next pitch.

And so on to the top . . . where, after coiling up the rope, you both find the easiest way down. This is usually a descent of grass and scree by the side of the crag, though sometimes it might go down an easy gully between two buttresses.

RUNNING BELAYS

On any rock where the leader feels there is a possibility he may slip, he attaches a sling either over a spike or round a chockstone or by inserting an artificial chockstone in the form of a small metal wedge (a *chock* or *nut*) on a small rope or wire loop. Then he clips the rope into the karabiner which belongs to that sling, loop or wire.

Now if he falls, and provided you lock off the rope in the stitcht plate with the chainsaw-starting action of the hand, he will fall the distance he is above the running belay and then the same distance below it. Providing, that is, the runner holds and does not break or become dislodged during the fall.

If the runner has been placed correctly, it will usually hold. It saves the climber a long fall.

The arts of belaying safely first, then runnering pitches effectively, are two skills every climber must possess. Even if you don't lead, it still falls to the second to 'clean' each pitch of the runners the leader has placed. This can sometimes prove infuriating, frustrating and fatiguing when chocks or nuts refuse to budge from awkwardly situated cracks. And there may be several recalcitrant runners on a pitch.

BRANCHING OUT ON YOUR OWN

When the time comes for you to start on easy classics with a friend who you hope will be your regular climbing partner, you can save money by pooling resources. It is the leader who requires most of the equipment taken on a rock climb. The person climbing second needs no more than their end of the climbing rope and the personal kit listed below.

*Individual Kit*   Apart from your track suit bottoms, thermals and sweat shirts, or shorts and T-shirt depending on the weather, you will also need your trainers for walking to the crag. You can even climb in trainers on the easier routes.

Specific rock climbing extras are: a climbing helmet which will protect your head from falling stones, dropped objects and accidental knockings against the rock and hard impacts when you fall head-first; a climbing harness with leg loops which allows you to sit comfortably when abseiling and at times when you might be suspended on the crag for various reasons; a stitcht plate with two slots in case you graduate to climb on two ropes rather than just the one and a screw-gate karabiner; a climbing nut extractor by which you lever and hook jammed nuts from cracks; a karabiner from which to hang the nut extractor on the harness ready for instant use; a pair of rock climbing shoes as light as trainers but with special soles of hard smooth rubber that give excellent friction with the rock; a figure-of-eight descendeur and screw-gate karabiner, again to hang on your harness ready for instant use; and a piece of old towel for drying greasy footholds.

*Communal Equipment*   The main piece of gear on which you can share the cost is the rope. Kernmantel (*perlon*) is best, fifty metres an ideal length, and the 11 mm full-weight thickness the safest you can buy.

Whoever leads carries the rest of your joint investment, of which the first and foremost item is the rock climbing guidebook covering the particular cliff where you happen to be.

Then come: several stitched nylon tape slings worn together like a bandolier over the head and one shoulder and each with a karabiner clipped to it; a bandolier sold specially for carrying wired nuts and karabiners worn across the opposite shoulder; nuts on short rope loops and wires clipped to the bandolier and ready for immediate use each with its own karabiner.

On many occasions a nut on a wire placed in a crack as a running belay will not be enough. It requires extending or it will be lifted out by the action of the climbing rope dragging the karabiner outwards and up as the leader climbs. An extra which helps is a number of small-size nylon tape extender loops which can be used for this purpose when you do not wish to use up all your longer tape slings.

Designs of metal chocks are constantly changing. They range from tiny micro-nuts little bigger than blobs of metal to the larger and mechanically-ingenious 'friends' which lodge in cracks with an amazing camming action.

The more you climb, the more you will be aware of the very specialized nature of modern rock climbing protection. How to use it effectively can only come with personal practice.

The bandolier method of racking your wires and so on, I must add, is my own preference. There are other methods, like clipping the wires and short loops with their nuts to your harness around the waist.

*Leading Safely*   Branching out on your own means choosing who is to lead climbs. The best way of all is to share the leads of alternate pitches, but there are successful partnerships where one person leads all the time and the partner is content to second permanently.

The guidebook is your helping hand. It gives a print-out of the climbs on each crag in its area, detailing their difficulty, height, length of pitches and the nature of the difficulties you can expect. It will also tell you the easiest way down.

The standards of difficulty are: Easy, Moderate, Difficult, Very Difficult, Severe, Very Severe and Extremely Severe. Starting from the bottom you may quickly find the Easies and

Moderates too simple. So the Diffs and V. Diffs are your next step up, but only when you really feel confident.

Then come the Severes and V Ss. If you find these so hard that you succeed in climbing them but at times feel frightened, it would be wise not to ignore this warning. It could mean you are climbing over your head. Go back down a grade of difficulty or two and work up some more experience until you finally feel happy on the harder climbs. It takes more time with some people than with others. You can only go by your own feelings. They are your best guide to safety.

Work your way up the grades of difficulty prudently and you will find the careful approach works wonders. There are many excellent classic climbs to choose from that are well documented. With the soundness of modern equipment and commonplace technique, rock climbing is a deservedly popular pastime.

## ICE CLIMBING

Climbing steep, and even overhanging, ice is different from rock climbing in one respect. The climbing involves a number of factors which are often out of your control. These are objective dangers which simply do not affect summer rock climbing, and because of them *the only safe way to begin is either with an outdoor centre specializing in winter climbing or with an experienced mountaineer.*

Statistics show that mountain accident rates are at their highest in winter. When you look at some of the objective dangers it is not, perhaps, surprising.

For example, belays become scarce because snow and ice lie thickly over the surface of the crag face and seal them off completely; the belays you will mostly use are ice screws which are not dependable unless you have experience of using them; because belays are harder to locate, the rope run-outs for pitches tend to become longer and with fewer running belays in between; avalanches are likely during or just after heavy snowfalls; cornices can collapse straight down the line of a gully ice route; because you have to wait for long spells in Arctic surroundings as you pass the rope through the stitcht plate while your partner leads, the bitter cold has more time to work you over while the body's muscles are no longer generating the warmth they do when you are climbing; the weather can change for the worse, catching you mid-route; winter's daylight hours are notoriously shorter than summer's; a section of ice may prove rotten, leaving you to climb steep rock in crampons; a crampon strap may snap and the crampon work off the boot as you lead a steep pitch of ice; a barrage of blocks of ice and frozen snow will bombard the second belayed directly below the leader who is dislodging the debris with his or her axes (this means the second can be taken off guard because he has to keep his head down and avoid turning round in the face of the falling blocks); a falling leader can cause serious injury with the points of his axe and crampons if he or she is unlucky enough to land on top of the second belayed below; conditions on the summit may be so severe – with spindrift cutting down visibility to nil – that you may be unable to find the easy descent to the safer lower mountain slopes.

With so much possibly to go wrong, you may be excused for wondering why risk ice climbing in the first place. Yet ice climbing is enjoyable. If you have climbing in your blood there is no doubt it will appeal, possibly even more than rock climbing. So long as you realize the extra hazards entailed and make due provision for their happening, you should complete many classic ice routes with a good margin of safety in hand.

COLD CLIMBING KIT

If winter hill walking requires more thin layers of clothing and extra food and warm drink, ice climbing calls for more still. A heavier kind of cagoule or mountain jacket is needed for severe winter weather. A balaclava or thermal monkey-mask worn below your climbing helmet is another requisite. Thermal gloves below Dachstein mitts are a must. And a warm scarf helps to keep the spindrift (which manages to penetrate any tiny spaces at the fringe of your hood) from pouring down your neck like icy sugar.

This clothing is necessary for the ice climbing you do rather than the walking to reach the cragface. The principles of personal climate control apply just as much in winter as in summer. Be sure you don't overheat on the hill through wearing too many layers. Perspiration in excess will soak, and devalue, your clothing layers given half a chance. In mid-winter that's risky.

Plastic climbing boots are by far the warmest, most comfortable and rigidly secure footwear for ice climbing.

Rock climbing equipment is needed, including your rack of wired nuts in case you encounter rock. Rock gives the best anchor of all on an ice climb. You will be lucky to find it, but when you do be sure you make the most of it.

The kind of crampons I suggested for winter hill walking will be suitable for climbing in too: twelve-pointed and with two protruding points at the front of each crampon. And a good tip here: sharpen your crampon points regularly with a file. Do not use a powered grinder which weakens the temper of the metal.

The piece of winter hill walking gear which is odd-man-out for winter climbing is the walking-stick-length ice axe. Too long to swing overhead in narrow gullies where you can find good ice, the shape of its gently curved pick is also wrong.

Ice climbing depends on being able to pull up on the axe you hold in each hand. The picks of these are driven into the ice overhead by an arm swing resembling a tennis serve. Your axes need only reach from finger tips to elbow in length.

Just one backward and then forward swing of the arm should be sufficient. If the axe's pick is either curved with a dropped end to resemble a hook, or forms a beak jutting down at 55° to the handle, it will penetrate the ice and hold firm when you pull down with your knuckles close to the ice. A gently curving pick would not do this. Apply any weight and it would slide back from its placement.

The only thing to do is save up and make your choice from the many shapes and sizes of ice tools available today. Other climbers will give advice. Surveys of ice climbing gear in climbing magazines help, so will the staff in good outdoor shops.

One axe needs a hammer head for placing and removing ice screws and at times for hammering the other axe into hard-frozen snow. This can be shorter than your axe with its pick and conventional adze.

Try to avoid an axe which has a super-efficient pick for penetrating ice. Some of the more futuristic shapes will actually do this so well they are difficult to extract after each overhead placement. This is tiring on a long climb that is likely to prove strenuous in the first place.

Two important extras help. A nylon tape slung from the head of the ice axe to form a wrist loop big enough to slip over mitts and take your weight off steep pitches gives the effect of a hand reaching down to grasp your wrist and haul you higher just when you need the extra help.

A quick-draw holster on either side of your harness helps so you can slip either or both axes out of the way if, say, you have to climb a section of rock with hands and crampon points.

Lastly, the leader carries a selection of ice screws for belays. The drive-in kind placed by straight hammer blows hold well. Tubular screws can also be good but are difficult to place and can become frozen up after one placement. Ideally, you practise using them on nursery slopes where it is safe to place them and hold falls on them.

ICE CLIMBING SECRETS FROM THE EXPERTS

Among all the other things you will pick up from being in good company on your early ice climbs, the following are crucial.

*The Different Kinds of Ice*   Snow falls on British hills at or below temperatures of 0°C. Around 0°C it falls as wet, coalesced

The position
to go for when
in doubt with
only one
ice axe

*Front-pointing up steep Névé (hard snow) in ice climbing fashion. Also the single axe anchor position*

flakes until the temperature drops. Then you have sugar-fine powder snow which is blown into gullies and on to buttresses by the wind.

With the passing of time, the crystal structure of the fallen snow breaks down. It becomes more compacted. Melting in the warmth of the day and freezing again at night, the snow's matrix fills with water, freezes, thaws and gradually becomes beautiful snow-ice.

I say 'beautiful' because that is what it is to the climber. Snow-ice in good condition gives great climbing. The axe picks find a ready placement in its surface every time. Each single swing of the feet will also locate the crampon's front points in the slope without needing a second kick.

Freshly frozen water produces a brittle ice. This improves with prolonged meltings and freezings. It also changes structure and becomes tougher and more plastic as well as different shades of blue and green.

Britain's climate is so varied you might experience different ices on one climb: good, bad and indifferent. During some weeks only waterfalls may be frozen with little snow in evidence elsewhere.

*Gradings of Ice Climbs*   Guidebook gradings try to keep you in line as they do with rock climbs. The Scottish Winter System is the one in British use. It goes from *Grade 1* to *Grade 6*, from gullies of straightforward but perhaps steep snow (and possibly with cornices) and easy-angled buttresses to 'serious climbs with high technical difficulty'.

As a rock climber trying ice, you may well manage *Grade 3* ice climbs (the climb will contain at least one vertical ice pitch and several minor ones) within a short time of starting providing you are with somebody who knows their winter climbing.

*Self-Arrest with Ice Tools*   Practice-slope trials are necessary to learn how your short climber's axe is going to behave on steep slopes. The hooked or angled pick can stick into the slope so abruptly the axe is torn from your hands despite the sling (and for practising I suggest you remove this so you go about your training uncluttered).

It is during your unroped climb up the steep open slopes of hard-frozen snow, and descending similar ground following the climb, that you must be ready for falls. These slopes will seem alarmingly steep until you become used to them, and the grip that crampons give you.

*The Golden Rule*    Learning how to place your ice axe and ice hammer picks with the minimum of effort comes with practice.

More important is that you realize the danger in rushing out to try this exciting technique regardless of prevailing conditions. If it is unsafe on the hill, these conditions will be unpleasant to climb in. They should be avoided for this reason alone.

# 11

## *Caving and Potholing*

Everyone peers into their hands as if counting their change. But the setting is moorland, and you are shining hard-hat headlights into your fingers to make sure the bright disc of yellow light is reflected there, so that you know you are on main beam and not dipped headlight before you slip down what looks like a dustbin jammed among the rocks.

The 'dustbin' is an oil drum without a bottom. But it has a dustbin lid to help prevent earth and stones falling into the particular pothole shaft which is directly below. And it is your entry into your first potholing trip underground.

So begins one of the sessions on a novice's course at Whernside Cave and Fell Centre near Dent, run by the Yorkshire Dales National Park Committee. It's the only centre of its kind in the world, and introduces thousands of people each year from home and abroad to the delights of underground trips.

Here are the kinds of thing you would learn if lucky enough either to attend a course here, or alternatively go on an outdoor pursuits centre course where caving is part of the programme.

### WHERE THE CAVES ARE

The only places on earth which are inaccessible to man are the deepest oceans and the hidden world of caves. Although the technology to reach the deepest ocean bed will probably ensure this happens, exploration will always be on the move to seek out unknown cave passages. We have known the world's highest mountain for over a century, but we still do not know which is the deepest cavern – only the deepest known so far.

Major cave systems still wait to be discovered all over the world. They are known to exist, but cavers have to find the keys to unlock these doors. However, this can happen even during a weekend caving trip along popular subterranean passages. Suddenly someone pushes on through a hole hitherto unexplored. Success! A new realm of caverns waits on the other side.

Anything of any size underground is in limestone. This applies from the British Isles, where the main areas are the Yorkshire Dales, the Derbyshire Peak District, the Somerset Mendips and South Wales, to America which has the longest known cave in the world (the Mammoth-Flint Ridge System in Kentucky, which gives over 180 miles of passages so far explored in all directions).

The deepest cave in the world is currently the Gouffre de Jean Bernard near Samoens in the French Alps. At 1,455 metres, it is challenged by the Gouffre de la Pierre Saint Martin and its close neighbour, the Sima de las Puertas de Illamina (once known as BU56). Both are in the Pyrenees and there is a chance they could attain even greater depths.

Switzerland, Cuba, Austria, Russia, Spain, Yugoslavia and Poland also boast some of the longest underground systems in the world. And now superb and extensive caverns are coming to light in previously unexplored parts of Mexico, South America, New Guinea and China.

## HOW CAVES ARE FORMED

Water has acted as scissors to the dotted lines already marked out and scored in the limestone crust by ancient earth movements millions of years ago. It has cut along these faults and joints, cracks and fissures, its cutting edges wetted with weak carbonic acid from the atmosphere and vegetation before it soaked into the rock. As the limestone is really a massive tomb of shellfish skeletons – the sediment of early seas – the acid eats it, and the water scours it.

The following features result:

*caves* – horizontal passages with no vertical shafts needing wire ladders or ropes

*potholes* – rifts in the ground, sometimes linked by cave passages, and requiring wire ladders as well as techniques involving abseiling down and jumaring back up single ropes

*stalactites* – icicle formations caused by water seeping on roofs, the carbonic acid evaporating, and a build-up of lime deposit forming

*stalagmites* – the reverse; they grow up from the floor fed by drips from the stalactites above, so taking much longer to grow

*columns* – where stalactites and stalagmites meet

*dripstone curtains* – deposits in sheets draped on walls

*helictites* – stalactites with twig-like branches

*cave pearls* – lime deposits wrapped around a grain of sand, say, in a small pool fed by water drips. They are quite rare in popular caves, but you never know your luck

*rimstone pools* – series of small pools reefed with thin walls of lime deposit

*troglodytes* – these are real cave dwellers like transparent water lice, a quarter of an inch long, and 'springtails' – insects which jump on pools, sand and mud.


## HOW TO BEGIN EXPLORING CAVES

There is only one safe way. That is to go on a course at Whernside Centre or to an outdoor pursuits centre which offers caving. Failing that, do get in touch with a caving club secretary who may well arrange for you to cave with club members during a weekend meet in a limestone caving area.

The basic reason for this is because the centre or club

will have the equipment you need: boiler suits, plastic helmets (not, for instance, a miner's helmet made from compressed cardboard which falls to pieces under waterfalls) and metal batteries on belts – none of which are adversely affected by water.

Having attended a caving course or caving club meet is not in itself the complete answer, but it is a good start. The next step is to join a proper caving club and go with members during weekends when again you will be able to take advantage of the communal gear like wire ladders and ropes which you would otherwise never have access to.

I know because I have tried caving by improvising with candles, clothes lines and bicycle lamps. It is from these experiences that I can say categorically that ordinary torch batteries, candles and so on are dangerously unreliable underground.

Even the usual advice to go with like-minded friends is not enough when it comes to caving. You should only go with experts until you become experienced yourself.

## WHY CAVING IS DIFFERENT

Caving offers unusual problems. You cannot check out your route first from safe vantage points as you can if you intend to go gorge walking, rock climbing or canoeing. Nor can you be seen on the tricky bits if you get into trouble. Underground there is total darkness. An inky blackness of a kind rarely experienced elsewhere prevails, broken only by the introduction of artificial light. And, needless to say, caving gives unusual problems to rescue teams.

## PERSONAL KIT

Caving is a great activity for using up old clothing. Wear it below a boiler suit to keep you warm when wet and muddy.

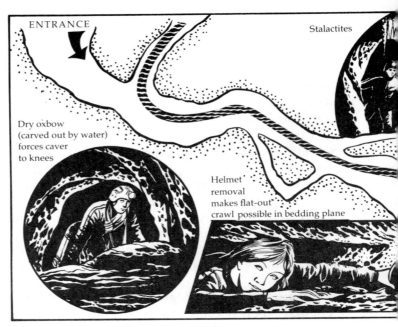

*Caving*

Your thermal underwear is fine, of course. But you can make do with anything made from wool. Worn next to the skin it is the best underclothing of all in wet systems. Layers of thin clothing on top are again ideal. If you get too hot – and it is possible – then you control your own climate by stripping off a layer or two. Pyjama trousers will make a good pair of substitute long johns.

Cavers wear short wellington boots with the kind of soles used on climbing footwear. They let water in, but the warmth of your body takes the chill off the water like an immersion heater. Alternatively you require strong lace-up boots with climber's type soles. Avoid boots with lace-hooks for potholing: the hooks catch on thin wire ladders.

Lastly, tie a whistle to the top buttonhole of your boiler suit. And check your helmet chinstrap is fastened firmly.

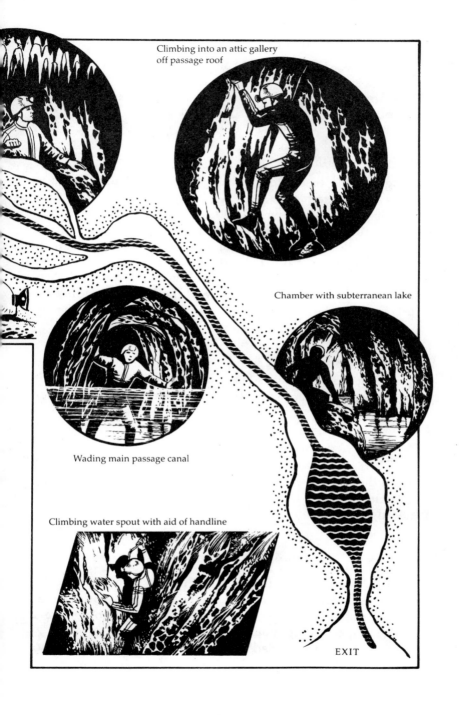

Climbing into an attic gallery off passage roof

Chamber with subterranean lake

Wading main passage canal

Climbing water spout with aid of handline

EXIT

## UNDERGROUND MOVEMENT

Here are some of the very basic ways of travelling underground.

### LADDER CLIMBING

Using whistle blasts to signal to the caver handling your safety rope (one blast = stop; two = take in; three = pay out) you descend the cobweb-like skeins hugging the wires, maintaining a bow-legged position that keeps your centre of gravity as close to the ladder as possible. Both hands grasp the ladder rungs from behind, while the boots alternate, treading the rungs with one boot feeling forward with the toe and the other, from the other side of the ladder, treading its rung with the heel.

### WADING

Splashing along passages chest-deep in water carrying a kit bag of wire ladders, not knowing if suddenly the water deepens . . .

### DUCKS

When the roof meets the water momentarily as when a large stalactite touches the pool below – you duck underneath holding your nose, getting completely soaked.

### CRAWLS

Cavers queue to pour themselves through tight places. The narrowest places demand you keep relaxed. Take your helmet off and push it through ahead, its headlamp shining like a garage inspection light at arm's length.

If others have wriggled through so can you. On a slot so tight that the helmet has to be removed, fully grown men and women can successfully pass through with careful breathing (only squeeze forward after you have exhaled).

Some crawls are wet. You might have to splash through on hands and knees with chin in the water and helmet scraping the ceiling. The bow wave created by the caver in front does not help.

If you feel stuck, rest. Patience pays here. You need to think like a contortionist and fit your body to the space available around you. Rather than tensing your body and trying to pull yourself through with the arms, push yourself forward with the toes of your boots.

### CLIMBING UNDERGROUND

All the problems that face rock climbers can be found underground. The cold, wet and dark make it a gripping experience, but on a safety rope you will be safe.

## CAVE SUCCESS AND SAFETY

It is not surprising that beginners whistle and sing underground to keep their spirits up. The enclosing darkness can be intimidating.

Thinking positively is the answer. If you are with experts; if your equipment is sound; if – like rock climbing – you are following a route described in a caving guidebook that is compatible in difficulty with your being a beginner (say, a *Difficult* cave rather than a *Severe* one); if you enjoy average fitness . . . then it will be possible.

It will also be safer. Experienced cavers will have let others on the surface know which cave they are exploring. They will also have checked the weather. To be trapped by flooding underground is a harrowing experience. However, if you are with others more experienced you have every chance of enjoying every moment. I hope you do.

# 12

## *Hang Gliding*

By law a hang gliding school cannot train anybody under the age of sixteen in the United Kingdom. Hang gliding has to be performed 'cold' from the beginning. There are no kindly nursery slopes as with rock climbing when it is time to go solo. You must utilize exactly the same thin air as the expert from your first solitary take-off.

That thin air gives substantial support when you know how to use it. A hang glider flies because of a very simple aerodynamic theory. Wind flowing over the curved surface of the wing or sail has slightly further to go than the air flowing below it. The air flowing across the top must accelerate so as to catch up the air below. Why? After its passage round the wing the air must reoccupy its original space in order not to leave a vacuum where the wing used to be.

This swifter-flowing air crossing the longer route over the top of the wing gets stretched out as a result. This lessens its pressure because pressure is proportional to the amount of air in a given location.

Since the air pressure on top of the wing is less than the air pressure beneath, the wing will try to move upwards, pressed by a force proportional to the difference in air pressure between the top and bottom. When the force is great enough the wing lifts and the hang glider flies.

The pilot must help nature along for this to happen. He or she must know the difference between airspeed and groundspeed. There is the angle of attack which is the angle the wing makes with the oncoming air and which you can control with your air speed so that by using the two you keep flying

and do not stall – the point at which there is no longer sufficient lift to support you in the air.

You must know when to push out on the control bar and when to pull it back in, when to lunge your body over to one side and when to swing it back over to the other.

There is a lot to hang gliding. It is easy to feel despair after your first few attempts. There are so many things to keep in mind and there seems such little time to act on them all before you make yet another crash-landing. It takes expert and sympathetic coaching, a certain amount of physical fitness and a determination to try, try and fly again.

This is why by law you need to wait until you are sixteen before you can enrol at a hang gliding school, which should be registered with the British Hang Gliding Association (BHGA).

You cannot buy a hang glider without attaining the Pilot One standard, nor will many clubs allow you to fly from their sites without it. Pilot One standard is something you can usually obtain after four to six flying days at a BHGA-registered school and having achieved it you will be able to start your progress through the Pilot Rating System.

## HANG GLIDING HISTORY

All the early aviation pioneers – including the Wright Brothers – piloted hang gliders. After all, that's what the early flying machines amounted to. Modern hang gliding, however, is one of the many spin-offs from the American space programme.

Dr Francis Rogallo originally developed the concept of a pointed parachute as a steerable recovery device for space craft. Although it was not used for this, flying enthusiasts in California, Australia and later Britain saw its potential as a means of achieving a lightweight one-man portable glider.

Early bamboo and polythene gliders soon gave way to gliders made from higher quality materials, with a corresponding increase in flying performance safety.

The most modern high performance hang gliders have achieved distances over 200 miles at heights exceeding 20,000 ft, for up to ten hours at a time.

## IS HANG GLIDING SAFE?

Hang gliding has come a long way since its early days. Hang glider designs have improved dramatically, higher quality materials are used and, most important of all, there are now hang glider pilots with several years' experience who can educate the newcomer to the sport and help him avoid the pitfalls that the pioneers of hang gliding had to face in their ignorance.

Thanks to improved training techniques, it is now an indisputable fact that to fly a hang glider in the 1980s is no more dangerous than any other adventurous sport, and actually safer than some.

## YOUR HANG GLIDER SCHOOLING

Read as much as you can find and digest of library hang gliding books. Join the BHGA, find out where the flying sites are and pay your local ones visits to watch what is happening. You can learn a great deal from chatting to pilots waiting their turn to fly or after flights and trying to analyse for yourself what is going on up there in the air.

Here are my own experiences of attending a BHGA course.

The instructor chalked arrows and tadpoles on a blackboard. The arrows represented things like lift, drag, thrust, weight. The tadpoles stood for the aerofoil of a hang glider wing seen as if looking end on at it. There were also tiny hang gliders at varying angles.

Questions rained at us during the theory session. 'So we know that knowing the difference between airspeed and groundspeed is important,' said the instructor. 'Like if we tread a moving walkway at 5 mph and it is already doing

5 mph, your airspeed is 5 mph but your groundspeed is 10 mph, the walkway standing for the air and the advertisements on the walls moving past the ground.

'But if you walk against the walkway at 5 mph, then your airspeed is 5 mph but your groundspeed is zero, and you are hovering as we frequently do when flying. OK?'

More examples followed. He asked us to picture a goldfish swimming at 5 mph in its bowl being carried across a room at 10 mph. In which direction would the water hit its face? The answer: the speeds are irrelevant, it would be hit on the face at whatever speed it swam and in whatever direction. Ditto hang glider pilot. The wind is always on your face whatever speed you travel and whether you fly against the wind or not.

SIMULATED FLIGHT

The instructor helped me on with the harness that had leg loops, a wooden seat and shoulder straps. Everything tightened up with a strap buckled across the stomach.

'Now,' he said, 'clip yourself on to the top of the control frame.' He indicated a large triangular A-frame made from strong alloy tubing pivoted from the ceiling, that took the place of the hang glider wing. This meant standing on a chair to reach high and clip the two remaining loops of harness webbing into the top of the A-frame with a karabiner – a manoeuvre not unlike a man preparing to hang himself! On stepping down I found my feet just touching the floor until I sat on the seat. Then I swung free.

Grasping the control bar at the bottom of the A-frame I found it easy to push it backwards and forwards as I swung to and fro.

'The control bar is fixed rigidly to the glider sail,' said the instructor. 'When you move the control bar you tip the wing up and down as well.'

Telling me to push out on the bar, he explained that this

made the nose lift to slow you down. Pull the bar in and the reverse happened; the nose dipped and you picked up speed.

I pushed and pulled in time with his 'go fasters' and 'slow downs', heartening to his 'coming on nicely', when out of the blue he rammed the bar at me saying: 'Quick! What do you do now?'

'You . . . you . . .' I gasped. The bar was jammed into my diaphragm like a teaspoon stabbing a teabag in hot water.

'You push it away!' He demonstrated. 'You fight back. You never let the glider control you. You don't just sit there. You tell it what to do.' And then he tore the bar so hard I let it slip from my fingers. 'Do something!' he said. I grabbed for the bar in vain.

'I should have pulled it backwards,' I said apologetically.

'You should indeed,' he said. 'OK, let's try again.' There followed ten minutes of combined arm wrestling and tug o' war, first one way then the other. This included constantly correcting the control bar to keep it level.

If one wing tip sank lower than the other, the instructor said, the glider would turn in that direction. To keep straight you had to throw your weight over to the other side and force down on that opposite end of the control bar. He slewed the A-frame in violent sideways jerks to drive this point home, saying: 'Get your backside over. You must learn to fly by the seat of your pants.'

I was mentally shattered when I finally stepped back on to the chair and unclipped the harness. We hadn't even left the building yet!

## SWANKSHOW

'*Swankshow!*' said the instructor, showing us how to assemble the gliders with safety checks to be made before each flight. Sail-wires-airframe-nose-king post. And *Show*? 'That's for the pilot,' he told us. Seat-helmet-observe wind. You go over everything with a fine-toothed comb.

TETHERED FLIGHT

Ropes were tied to either wing and the nose and one person holding each ran with the pilot. This gave the kite less chance of diving into the ground or soaring uncontrollably into the air. The aim of the first few flights was to achieve distance over the ground, not height, and to let us experience the 'feel' of hang gliding.

It worked well. The instructor held the nose line and talked us through. Other students managed the wing lines. We took it in turns to skim the grass, legs hanging limply below the great sail. It seemed no time at all before the legs were running on touch-down as you slowed the glider by pushing the control bar out and away from you.

SOLO FLIGHT

'OK?' said the instructor. 'Onetwothreerun!' And we did, we did! These were our first solo shots. The wing lifted like a big hat, your shoulders came free from the weight of the control frame you must carry in front of you during take-off and you felt your boots leave the ground. But as to actually flying? Uh-uh!

Sometimes I pulled the bar in too much and nosedived in a crumpled heap. Or I would push it away too hard, fail to fill the wing with air and run all the way downhill in moon-like bounds. Once the kite landed at such a pace I was dragged after it along the grass, hanging on to the control bar, knuckles mercifully saved by the two small wheels fitted on each end of the bar for training flights. And always I baulked when the glider veered to one side or the other, snatched this way and that by sudden gusts, despite the instructor's roars of 'Right . . . right . . . go to your right!' or 'Backside to the left . . . the *left*!' Yet he had told us it was always difficult at first because everything seemed to happen at once. And that, like learning to ride a bike, you spend a long time getting nowhere before things suddenly click. So perhaps there was still hope, forlorn as it looked. Already it was growing dark.

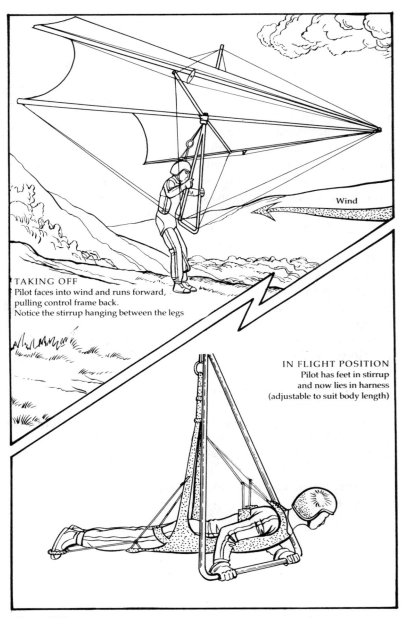

**TAKING OFF**
Pilot faces into wind and runs forward,
pulling control frame back.
Notice the stirrup hanging between the legs

Wind

**IN FLIGHT POSITION**
Pilot has feet in stirrup
and now lies in harness
(adjustable to suit body length)

*Hang gliding*

Lugging the glider back uphill, head and shoulders jammed through the opposite side of the control frame from flying position, was a fitness course in itself. No wonder the instructor looked fit. It was more than I did as I completed my umpteenth *swankshow* after yet another bodged flight and bad landing, track suit bottoms all cow muck, dead bracken and wet moss.

Yet it happened like he said, and before I'd even realized. One moment the heart-bumping-resigned-to-crashing take-off run; the next, the ground continued to unreel below my boot soles − a rock, snow patch, a dead sheep all flashing underneath − as if the talons of a golden eagle had me by the shoulders and were speeding me through the air at 20 mph (the speed we were told we would fly). And then I was down in my usual semi-crash landing. But very happy.

Thirty metres had the instructor said? It felt like triple that. And as for height, I'd been soaring. 'Actually, you were about a metre up,' he said, adding, 'Don't forget your head is two metres higher than your boots so it always seems higher off the ground than it is.'

Several more tiny hops followed. The instructor flew in competitions wearing a special 'holey' helmet so he could hear the wind noise; my crash hat had no such holes but his voice cut through like a loud-hailer. 'Be greedy! Push forward! Fight for every extra inch of air. We've had nobody in hospital yet!'

From such a beginning hang glider school students fly much higher solo carrying Civil Aviation Authority (CAA) and BHGA approved radios so the instructor can still keep in touch during each flight.

At this point you're heading towards the real thing: converting to flying prone with both feet tucked up behind you as the giant sail above cruises the skies to your command.

# 13

## *Small Boat Sailing and Boardsailing*

Cruising in a cutter between the mainland and Skye, I can vouch for the effect of a fast sail on my colleagues – boys and girls aged between sixteen and twenty (plus instructor). With the sheet pulled in, the boat bombed along, seemingly balanced on one half-buried gunwale. You felt you were pushing the boat over with your feet pressing on the duck-boards.

One schoolboy, unused to sailing, said: 'Hey, is this the normal angle?' Someone else replied deadpan: 'We're not out of the harbour yet, mate!'

It was amazing how quickly everyone got used to the sight of the masts leaning over the water. You soon ceased to wonder if the sea hissing along that plunging gunwale was going to keep its distance much longer. It was obviously going to.

Sailing or boardsailing, there's nothing to compare with either if you are a young person addicted to cranking over at sharp angles on a large expanse of water, letting the wind power you in the direction where your heart most wants to be at minimum further cost.

The owner of a small boat or sailboard is fortunate in this respect. Having purchased your craft, your remaining outlay is something like twenty times less in comparison with, say, downhill skiing, water skiing or sub-aqua diving. And that is taking depreciation and the costs of getting to the water into account.

There are many different kinds of small boat. If you cannot afford to buy one for some time, look on it as a blessing in disguise. Because of the choice available you might have ended up with something that is satisfactory in the first instance, but which quickly gets more unsuitable as your experience grows.

It is a better idea to gain experience first, then buy the boat or board which you know would suit you most over a long-term period.

In the meantime perhaps I can give you a glimpse of the good things that wait the young sailor or wind surfer and the basic ways of getting on the water without possessing either of these kinds of craft.

## SMALL BOAT SAILING

You may know nothing about small boat sailing but you can pick up the rudiments by making friends with sailors during a holiday at any popular seaside resort.

Any of the bronzed boatmen who earn their living in summer by taking holiday-makers out sailing know that most people are attracted either by the novelty of the thing, or merely by the idea of enjoying the breeze on a hot day. But if one of the party is really interested, most boatmen will be willing to let him or her try a hand at the tiller.

Another way of getting on the water is to go on a sailing course, but before you do even this perhaps you know, or can get to know, somebody with a dinghy who will take you out in the craft.

### SAILING A DINGHY

If you can sail a dinghy successfully, you can sail a family cutter. If you can sail a family cutter, you can sail the next size of boat up, and so on.

Most sailing schools use dinghies for instruction afloat and there is much sense in this. Once you can handle one of these confidently the move up to something larger will be easy to make. In the sailing programme of Outward Bound schools they sail 26-ft cutters, but the students also experience handling dinghies on estuary waters first.

It is said that good boatsailors are born and not made. It certainly helps if you have a steady nerve, a light touch and an inside that is not disturbed by the movement of a boat. Swimming should be added to the qualifications. If you cannot swim you should not attempt to sail a boat on your own.

*The Language of Sailing*   You may find it interesting to pick up the terms used in sailing, and any practical hints you can, before setting sail.

In any boat, for instance, the left and right sides when looking forward are called 'port' and 'starboard'. But with sails set one speaks also of the 'weather' and 'lee' sides of the boat, which vary according to the side the wind is coming from. And under sail, besides the common terms 'ahead' and 'astern', 'forward' and 'aft', one also refers to the wind to indicate direction. Thus 'to windward' is the direction from which the wind blows, the opposite direction being 'to leeward'. 'Near the wind' means a direction nearly facing the wind; 'away from the wind' refers to directions turning more away from it. To point directly at the wind is to point 'into the wind's eye'.

Your dinghy will probably have two sails – the foremost one called the foresail or jib; the other, the mainsail. The ropes used in the boat for hauling the two sails aft or for easing them to allow them to belly out over the sides are called the 'sheets'. One of the first rules of boatsailing is that the main sheet should never be secured, but kept in hand in the event of a sudden squall or a strong gust of wind.

You will discover there are three ways of sailing: 'running free' directly before the wind with both sheets eased well out; 'reaching' with the wind on one side or the other and the sheets hauled further in; and sailing 'close-hauled', with the wind nearly ahead and both sheets hauled in so as to flatten the sails.

When running free the boat remains level, and there is no weather or lee side. The steersman can sit whichever side he likes, but when reaching or sailing close-hauled the boat heels over in the wind and he then always sits up on the weather side.

Reaching is the easiest form of sailing. All you have to do is steer the boat steadily in the direction you wish to go. When running free the boat is always inclined to yaw about from side to side and, if you are not careful, the sails which are bellying out almost at right-angles to the boat may suddenly swing violently across to the other side. This is called a 'gybe'. Except that the boom may at best knock your hat off or at worst crack you on the head, it is harmless in light winds. But if the wind is blowing at all freshly, it is a common form of capsize.

When close-hauled you sail as close to the wind's eye as you can. This is the most difficult form of sailing. Naturally no boat will sail exactly head-on to the wind, but if kept a small angle away from it, the sails, stretched flat aft by the sheets, will keep full of wind and push the boat ahead.

You do not steer in any fixed direction. Your object is to steer so that both sails will keep *just* full of wind, and no closer to it than that, or they will begin shaking and the boat will come to a stop. Close-hauled with the wind on the starboard side you are on the starboard tack and on the port tack if the wind is on the port side.

To 'beat to windward' means making a zigzag course towards the wind's eye by a series of tacks either way. After each tack the boat is turned around head to wind on the other tack, and this progress, during which both sheets are hauled over to the other side, is called 'going about'. If instead of filling her sails on the other tack, the boat sticks in the wind's eye with her sails shaking, it is called 'missing stays' or 'being in irons'.

If by reason of a rough sea or bad sailing a boat refuses to go about, she may always be got round on to the other tack by turning round the other way, stern to the wind. This is called 'wearing'. The sheets are gradually eased out and the boat kept away until she is running free. The sheets are then shifted over and hauled in again as she comes up to the wind on the other tack.

When passing stern to wind, the main sheet must be very carefully tended so as to avoid any sudden jerk when gybing. If blowing fresh it is often safest to take in the mainsail just before the gybe, and set it again directly afterwards.

When you can sail the boat close-hauled, put her about and wear her round yourself, you are getting on. And if the boatman or sailing school instructor sees you are really keen, he will be glad to teach you more about it.


## BOARDSAILING

Windsurfing, unlike small boat sailing, allows room for only one person on board at one time. You have to sail solo, but there is no need to be alone. The success rate of certified windsurfing schools is so high you could well be one of the 90 per cent of novices who learn in four to six hours. Then the world of rough water sailing – storm sailing, in fact – becomes a possibility. It is on mountainous waves driven by high winds that the sailboard comes into its own when handled by an expert.

As that embryo boardsailor with a few hours' practice, light winds and calm water will be your style. Become expert and you go on from there to drive your board through the kind of seas that make most pleasure boat sailors run for shore.

Statistics show that the safety rate is one of the highest in great outdoors activities. The board and rig are sufficiently light to be carried a considerable way to the water by fairly small people, say twelve-year-olds. The lighter you are, the better for windsurfing. It means less resistance, allowing you to travel quickly. Accelerate more and the board lifts further out of the water to give you an extra advantage.

Boardsailing has come a long way since its beginnings in the late 1950s. Today it is the latest Olympic sport and has become a multi-million pound business. Certified windsurfing schools are part of this growth industry. They are certainly the answer for most people on their own who have no other access to a sailboard and expert instruction.

FIRST STEPS IN WINDSURFING

As you climb aboard your first sailboard, the first thing to suffer will be your pride. Most beginners can expect to fall in every two or three minutes during their debut on water. The next thing you feel are muscle pains – in the arms first, then the legs and finally all over.

The good news is that it takes no longer than a couple of minutes to fully rig and set up a board usually made of plastic or fibreglass, about 4 m (12ft) long and weighing, say, 18 kg (40 lb.). On the water it will sport a small daggerboard keel to prevent it blowing off to the side.

The mast will be made from spun fibreglass or aluminium weighing approximately 4 kg (8 lb.) and fitting on to a universal joint that also attaches to a moulded slot in the board. The sail slips over the mast. It is kept extended one way by the mast and acrossways by a wishbone boom.

It is by grasping the wishbone and moving it along with mast and sail that the windsurfer holds the rig up, steers without help from a rudder and is also supported.

Here is how it works. Dinghy and sailboard sails act like a hang glider sail. Wind pressure inflates the sail into a wing-like aerofoil shape. As we saw with the hang glider, a pressure differential is caused by air flowing over the curved surfaces. And the boat or board is drawn towards the low-pressure area as a result.

To prevent the boat or board being drawn sideways, a plate of wood or plastic called a centreboard or daggerboard projects down into the water beneath. This allows the board or sailboard to slice forward but greatly reduces sideways movement.

The difference between a boat and sailboard is that a boat has a rudder to make it turn by deflecting the water underneath. A sailboard has a movable mast. The fact that the mast moves this way and that makes a rudder unnecessary on a sailboard.

If you tip the sail forwards when standing with your back to the wind, the nose of the sailboard will swing around until

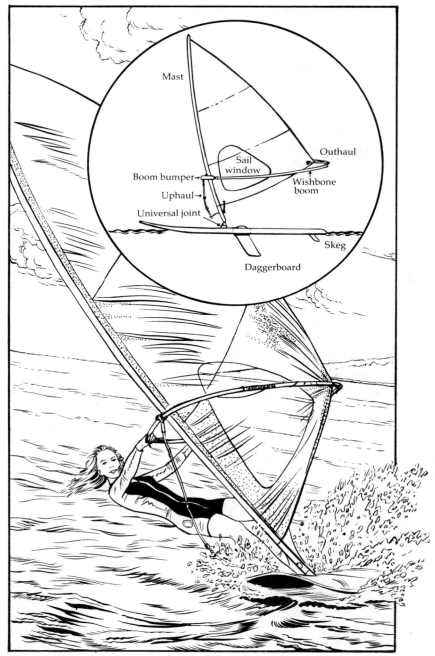

Mast

Outhaul

Sail window

Boom bumper→

Wishbone boom

Uphaul→

Universal joint

Skeg

Daggerboard

*Windsurfing*

it points away from and in line with the wind. On the other hand, tip the sail back and the nose will swing round as if trying to point into the eye of the wind and in line with it.

You will pick up the theory behind this from books on boardsailing or at boardsailing school. It concerns the relationship of the centre of lateral resistance (CLR) – the theoretical point on the board from which it would be possible to push or pull the craft sideways at right angles – and the centre of effort (CE) in the sail. This is the theoretical point of the sail through which the sum of all the forces produced by a sail acts, and is not the same as the geometric centre of the sail which does not alter. If you move the CE in front of the CLR, the nose pivots away from the wind as we have seen by tipping the sail forward. But do the opposite, and move the CE behind the CLR, and the front of the board will pivot round towards the wind again as we have seen by tipping the sail back.

There is more to it than raking the sail forward and back. To turn a sailboard downwind efficiently you not only rake the sail forward but sheet the sail in too. To turn the board upwind you do the reverse: rake the sail back and sheet the sail out so its front part is not filled with air and is said to be 'luffed'. Sufficient to say for now that with this very basic knowledge you can take your first steps at a windsurfing school.

You will not only learn the theory in full detail, but be taught how to boardsail correctly. Learn on your own or with friends and the sad fact is that you will pick up bad habits and wrong techniques that tend to remain with you for good.

Boardsailing instructors teach you the best methods which you will not learn going it alone or on a friend's board. Learning to stand straight on the board is one of the first things to master. The beginner who is not schooled differently tends to stick his bottom out as he sails. This is a bad stance and is the frequent cause for capsizes even when you have learned to sail.

Another classic mistake is often made getting under way. Standing sideways on the board, back to the wind and sail before moving across the water, the windsurfer must pull the rig up using both hands on the uphaul rope until the wishbone boom is swinging free in the wind just above the water.

The beginner will invariably grasp the boom with both hands and try to draw the rig up, yet unless the mast is in exactly the right position, the sail will luff up and the nose veer round into the wind.

Windsurf course students wonder why they are coached the seemingly complicated starting-off method of crossing their mast hand (forward) over the other hand (sail) to grasp the boom before moving the sail hand into position further down the boom. But it is all to improve control, and especially to allow the mast to be tilted forward before the sail is harnessed to the wind to prevent luffing.

Such are the countless details that are ironed out on your course. They have to be if you are going to continue board-sailing with any real purpose. As an expert says: 'You can get away with wrong techniques in light winds, but not in strong.'

But then the differences between a sailing boat and a sailboard are not significant in light winds. It is in winds of force 4 or greater that a sailboard comes into its own. At force 4 the wind speed is 13–18 mph or 11–16 knots and it means small waves with many whitecaps evident on the surface of the water. At force 6 where the wind is blowing at 25 knots or so there are large waves, whitecaps everywhere and spray. These are just the kinds of conditions where a sailboard cannot usually be beaten on any point of sail by a boat that does not have at least twice the sailboard's sail area.

For this kind of windsurfing your technique must be sound. A certified windsurfing school will give you the best start towards gaining this exciting and rewarding level.

# 14

## *Broadening Your Horizons*

'You can't be too careful,' they say. But it's just as true to say that you cannot succeed without exposing yourself to risk. Both these maxims apply when you are ready to visit where the action is – wild, rugged countryside is very different from the surroundings you are used to at home.

It's easy to get too confident. This happens when we find adventure pursuits are not as impossible as we at first imagined – rock faces provide grips for hands and feet, river rapids give us resting places in the shape of eddies circling among the foam and caves are not the mantraps parents always imagine. It's a heady discovery. Modern adventure equipment and clothing look and feel good. And so, it's easy to imagine, do we when using and wearing it.

The safest way to go about adventurous activities is when you have experience, yet there has to be an element of risk if you are going to learn. Where do you draw the line?

## GAINING EXPERIENCE

A safe way to begin is at an outdoor pursuits centre which teaches the basics of the activities in this book – though few centres cover them all. Hundreds of thousands of young people enjoy this kind of start each year. You are shown the ropes by instructors who know what they are doing. Safety rules apply all the way and equipment is the best. You soon come to appreciate the fact as you dangle on the end of a rope!

In certain outdoor activities a course is the only way. Hang gliding, for example. Too much is at stake when you take off and are left to your own devices, still a raw beginner. There were many accidents in the early days of hang gliding because this approach did not exist.

You must strike a balance when it comes to risk. On the one hand you don't take needless chances; on the other, if you don't take calculated risks – as when you do a rock climb – you'll never get the most out of the great outdoors.

Remember: whether you start at an adventure school like Outward Bound or take up your adventure-sport with friends, you might do well to heed the words of a celebrated mountaineer – 'We did it in easy stages, gaining confidence and experience as we went along.'

## LEARNING PATIENCE

The all-consuming desire to rush off to the hills or sea immediately, once the bug has bitten, is natural. It is also dangerous if you don't stop to think about it first.

It is the reason you can be tempted to over-reach yourself in hikes, climbs and voyages that are really too tough for you. Time is short; you've come a long way by car; you must at least try what you've set your hearts on . . . Or so the risky logic goes.

It even happens to experienced mountaineers.

Winter after winter in the Scottish Highlands see climbers caught in avalanches in big mountain gullies which offer some of the best ice climbing in the world, and the majority of these are English.

'It's not that climbers from south of the border aren't used to our conditions,' an instructor from Glenmore Lodge says. 'It's because there are so many of them. There is bound to be numerical risk with such large numbers – except for one thing.

'While Scottish climbers may go to the pub in bad conditions because they can come back the following week, the

English climber might push his luck. He's come a long way, snow and ice doesn't last for ever and he feels he has to take his chances.'

And one of the greatest climbers, who has climbed the North Wall of the Eiger and Everest, says: 'I've got more scared as I grow older. I'm alive now because from the very start I've always been cautious and never worried what people will say if I turn back.

'I've been in dozens of situations when you know if you make one mistake you will fall off and get killed. I tell you quite frankly I don't enjoy it.

'But I'll tell you this. There are dozens of people who come up here /Ben Nevis in winter/ with absolutely no idea of the danger . . .

'If you can climb Ben Nevis you can climb anywhere in the world. It is as hard as that but tragically there are those who won't believe it because Ben Nevis isn't the Himalayas.'

Impatience can be a killer.

## ACCLIMATIZING PARENTS

Parents are often reluctant to let their children venture into the wilds with friends as inexperienced as themselves. And who can blame them? To many the great outdoors seems hostile and dangerous, and parents may be understandably fearful for your safety.

The best way to get parents – and others who care for you – on your side is to show how genuinely interested you are in wild country adventure.

Borrow library books on the activities which grip you and buy the ones that really appeal. Subscribe to outdoor magazines. In these you'll find the addresses of equipment manufacturers offering catalogues to all who write to them. Some are free, for others you pay a small fee.

Certain outdoor adventure equipment catalogues and brochures are works of art, and their illustrations make first-class wall posters. You will also find ads for posters in outdoor magazines. These, along with Ordnance Survey maps, are great for bedroom walls too.

You will be able to read advance notices of public lectures – with illustrations – given by famous mountaineers, long-distance walkers, sailors and so on at various large towns and cities through the winter lecturing season. An autographed copy of that celebrity's book bought and signed at the lecture would be another arrow to your bow. So would a picture postcard sent to you from a Himalayan climbing expedition base camp and signed by all the climbers on that trip! This is sometimes possible if you make a small donation to that venture; it's a way of raising expedition funds sometimes advertised in climbing periodicals.

Then there are addresses of adventure schools like Outward Bound, Glenmore Lodge, Plas y Brenin and so on, not to mention training schemes such as those of the British Canoe Union Coaching Scheme. Nor should you forget the list of outdoor clubs specializing in the kind of thing which interests you – all you have to do is write to the secretary at the address provided.

Some outdoor pursuit centres occasionally run 'Fathers and Sons' courses. What better way to get parents interested than to go sailing, mountain walking and rock climbing with them! It's as good a way as any to put their minds at rest.

The Duke of Edinburgh's Award Scheme in the United Kingdom say that where outdoor activities are concerned they make a special point of stressing the need to train properly before you actually try any of the outdoor pursuits they cover. Parents of those taking the Award Scheme should be reassured to know of the safety precautions taken, which have been tightened up still further after recent criticism by mountain-rescue teams.

Finally, ask your parents for birthday and Christmas presents that reflect your interest in the great outdoors. You might even persuade them to help pay for you to attend a short adventure school course. It's easier for them to urge caution but still let you go if they have staked a claim with your equipment or clothing, or even your initial training.

Never forget that real safety on hills, on rivers, on the sea and in the sky can't be bought; it can only come from your own personal experience of doing things in easy stages, and parents are more likely to let you go ahead when they know you go along with this thinking.

APPENDIX 1

# *First Aid*

## FIRST AID BASICS

There are three main rules for outdoors first aid:
1. Don't panic. (You might be surprised how many people do, including adults.) Try to sum up the situation as quickly as possible.
2. First things first – deal with essentials.
3. Telephone for help, sending two messengers while someone stays with the casualty.

The essentials keep the casualty alive, even though he or she may be in bad shape. They are your main concern.

*Rescue Breathing* Lay the casualty face up; clear the mouth and throat with a finger; tilt the head back *as far as possible*; pinch the nostrils; take a deep breath; cover the mouth with your own and blow, making the chest rise; move your face away so that the casualty can breathe out, and watch the chest fall. Repeat until the casualty can breathe alone, keeping the head tilted back as far as possible all the time.

*Bleeding* Grasp the sides of the wound and firmly press them together; lay the casualty down, if possible with the injured part above the level of the heart; apply firm pressure with fingers or a pad for at least ten minutes to allow the blood to clot (if you have no dressing, use a clean handkerchief, folded T-shirt or whatever); then pad and bandage firmly but not so much as to stop the circulation; *never* remove the first pad but add extra padding on top if the bleeding continues. Always remember that even a little blood looks like a lot.

*Broken Bones*   Inspect the limbs for tenderness or swelling, and for anything out of shape (don't try to make the casualty stand up for a quick test to see if a leg is broken! – if in any doubt, tie the injured leg to the other leg with padding in between). If an arm is injured, tie it to the side *in the most comfortable position.*

Don't worry about splints. Just concentrate on keeping the casualty as still and comfortable as possible.

*Shock*   Give warmth, comfort and reassurance in every accident (people die from untreated shock); allow fresh air to circulate; loosen tight clothing; insulate the casualty from the cold ground; put the casualty inside a sleeping bag or plastic survival bag; raise the feet a little; *don't* give anything to eat or drink if you suspect internal injuries in case an anaesthetic is needed in the next four hours (otherwise warm sweet drinks help to revive the person suffering from shock).

The key things are: WARMTH, COMFORT, REASSURANCE.

*Exposure* or *Hypothermia*   Caused by wet, cold or exhaustion. Watch out for companions stumbling, swearing, complaining of tiredness, not being able to see, becoming incoherent, growing pale-faced and behaving unusually; take them to lower ground and shelter.

Do *not* force them to keep moving. Do *not* rub, chafe or use hot water. Do *not* remove wet clothing.

Put them in a sleeping bag or survival bag; possibly get inside with them; pitch some form of shelter. If they can still eat, give them sugary food, sweets or glucose tablets.

# APPENDIX 2

# *A Selection of Outdoor Pursuit Centres*
(see also list of *Useful Addresses*)

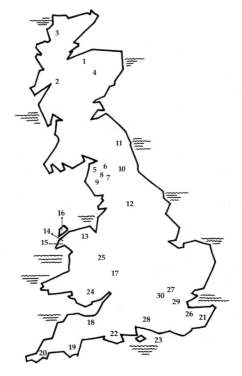

**1** Glenmore Lodge
National Outdoor Training
Centre
Aviemore
Inverness-shire PH22 1QU

**2** Outward Bound Loch Eil
Achdalieu
By Corpach
Fort William
Inverness-shire

3   John Ridgway Adventure
      School
    Ardmore
    Rhiconich
    By Lairg
    Sutherland 1V27 4HB

4   Highland Guides
    Inverdruie
    Aviemore
    Inverness-shire PH22 1QH

5   Outward Bound Eskdale
    Eskdale Green
    Holmrook
    Cumbria CA19 1TE

6   Outward Bound Ullswater
    Ullswater
    Penrith
    Cumbria

7   Whernside Cave and Fell
      Centre
    Dent
    Sedbergh
    Cumbria LA10 5RE

8   Brathay Hall
    Ambleside
    Cumbria LA22 0HP

9   YMCA National Centre
    Lakeside
    Ulverston
    Cumbria LA12 9BD

10  Malham Tarn Field Centre
    Settle
    North Yorkshire BD24 9PU

11  Windy Gyle Outdoor Centre
    West Street
    Belford
    Northumberland NE70 7QE

12  Peak National Park Study
      Centre
    Losehill Hall
    Castleton
    Derbyshire

13  Plas y Brenin
    National Centre for
      Mountain Activities
    Capel Curig
    Betws-y-Coed
    Gwynedd

14  Outward Bound Wales
    Aberdovey Centre
    Aberdovey
    Gwynedd
    Wales

15  Outward Bound Wales
    Rhowniar Centre
    Tywyn
    Gwynedd
    Wales

16  Plas Menai Outdoor Centre
    Caernarfon
    Gwynedd
    Wales

17   PGL Young Adventure Ltd
Station Street
Ross-on-Wye
Herefordshire HR9 7AH

18   Dartmoor Expedition
Centre
Widecombe-in-the-Moor
Devon

19   Drake's Island Adventure
Centre
Mayflower Centre
Plymouth
Devon PL2 3DG

20   Compass West
Sennen
Cornwall

21   Bowles Outdoor Centre
Tunbridge Wells
Kent TN3 9LW

22   Poole Sailing and
Boardsailing Schools
43 Panorama Road
Sandbanks
Poole
Dorset

23   Isle of Wight Hang Gliding
Training Centre
Rose Cottage
Clay Lane
Newbridge
Isle of Wight

24   Welsh Hang Gliding Centre
New Road
Crickhowell
Powys
South Wales

25   Welsh Hang Gliding Centre
17 Well Street
Ruthin
Clwyd
North Wales

26   Skyriders British Hang
Gliding School
15 St Mary's Green
Biggin Hill
Kent

27   Dunstable Hang Gliding
School Ltd
55 Spring Lane
Great Horwood
Milton Keynes MK17 0QP

28   Hampshire Flight Training
Centre
21 Penns Road
Petersfield
Hampshire

29   London Sailboards
101 The Chase
London SW4

30   Peter Chilvers Windsurfing
78 Norbury Road
Thornton Heath
Surrey

# APPENDIX 3

# *Useful Addresses*

The Ramblers Association
1/5 Wandsworth Road
London SW8 2JJ

Backpackers' Club
20 St Michaels Road
Tilehurst
Reading
Berkshire

Long Distance Walkers
   Association
4 Mayfield Road
Tunbridge Wells
Kent TN4 8ES

The Camping Club of Great
   Britain and Ireland Ltd
11 Lower Grosvenor Place
London SW1W 0EY

British Canoe Union
Flexel House
45/47 High Street
Addlestone
Surrey KT15 1JV

Scottish Canoe Association
18 Ainslie Place
Edinburgh EH3 6AU

Welsh Canoeing Association
Pen-y-Bont
Corwen
Clwyd LL21 0EL

Canoe Association of Northern
   Ireland
2A Upper Malone Road
Belfast
Northern Ireland BT9 6LA

Cyclists' Touring Club
Cotterell House
69 Meadrow
Godalming
Surrey GU7 3HS

British Cyclo-Cross Association
15 Lyndhurst Avenue
Hazel Grove
Stockport
Cheshire

187

The Rough-Stuff Fellowship
(Cyclo-Cross Touring)
51 Hurst Drive
Stretton
Burton-on-Trent
Staffordshire DE13 0EB

The Fell Runners Association
165 Penistone Road
Kirkburton
Huddersfield
West Yorkshire HD8 0PH

British Orienteering Federation
41 Dale Road
Matlock
Derbyshire DE4 3LT

National Caving Association
c/o Whernside Cave and Fell
Centre
Dent
Sedbergh
Cumbria LA10 5RE

British Mountaineering Council
Crawford House
Precinct Centre
Booth Street East
Manchester

The Mountaineering Council of
Scotland
59 Morningside Park
Edinburgh

Association of British Mountain
Guides
64 Barco Avenue
Penrith
Cumbria

International School of
Mountaineering
Club Vagabond
1854 Leysin
Switzerland

Ski Club of Great Britain
118 Eaton Square
London SW1W 9AF

British Hang Gliding
Association
Cranfield Airfield
Cranfield
Bedfordshire MK43 0YR

The Royal Yachting Association
Victoria Way
Woking
Surrey GU21 1ED
*(Ask for a list of registered*
*windsurfing schools, too)*

South East Boardsailing
Association
Ryetops
Matts Hill Road
Hartlip
Sittingbourne
Kent

Holiday Fellowship Ltd
140–144 Great North Way
London NW4 1EG

YHA Adventure Holidays
Trevelyan House
St Albans
Hertfordshire

YHA (England and Wales)
14 Southampton Street
London WC2

Scottish YHA
7 Glebe Crescent
Stirling FK8 2JA

Duke of Edinburgh Award
   Scheme
5 Prince of Wales Terrace
London W8

Outward Bound Trust
12 Upper Belgrave Street
London SW1X 8BA